DOUBT

A Road to Growth

DOUBT

A Road to Growth

JACKIE HUDSON

Here's Life Publishers

Published by
HERE'S LIFE PUBLISHERS, INC.
P. O. Box 1576
San Bernardino, CA 92402-1576

HLP Product Number 951855
© 1987 Here's Life Publishers
All rights reserved.
Printed in the United States of America

Library of Congress Cataloging-in-Publication Data
Hudson, Jackie, 1949-
    Doubt, a road to growth.

    Bibliography: p.
    1. Belief and doubt.   2. Hudson, Jackie, 1949-
I. Title.
BV4637.H79   1987   231'.042   86-33666
ISBN 0-89840-186-0 (pbk.)

Unless otherwise indicated, Scripture quotations are from the *New American Standard Bible,* © The Lockman Foundation 1960, 1962, 1963, 1968, 1971, 1972, 1975, 1977, and are used by permission. Other Scripture quotations are from the King James Version (KJV).

FOR MORE INFORMATION, WRITE:

L.I.F.E. — P.O. Box A399, Sydney South 2000, Australia
Campus Crusade for Christ of Canada — Box 300, Vancouver, B.C., V6C 2X3, Canada
Campus Crusade for Christ — Pearl Assurance House, 4 Temple Row, Birmingham, B2 5HG, England
Campus Crusade for Christ — P.O. Box 240, Colombo Court Post Office, Singapore 9117
Lay Institute for Evangelism — P.O. Box 8786, Auckland 3, New Zealand
Great Commission Movement of Nigeria — P.O. Box 500, Jos, Plateau State Nigeria, West Africa
Campus Crusade for Christ International — Arrowhead Springs, San Bernardino, CA 92414, U.S.A.

With deep appreciation
I dedicate this book to my friends

NEY BAILEY
MARY GRAHAM
KAREN PETERSON
CAROLYN REXIUS

who walked with me
through my darkest times of doubt and pain.
Thank you!

CONTENTS

CONTENTS

FOREWORD

For every confirmed skeptic I encounter, I meet at least a dozen sincere believers who struggle with doubt. At times their apprehension is casual, but at others it is grave. These people want to believe God but, for whatever reason, wrestle with thoughts and feelings to the contrary. And, unfortunately, when doubt enters the believer's experience, it threatens to paralyze him. I have found a book to recommend to just such a person.

This book tackles the problem head-on and with absolute candor. In *Doubt: A Road To Growth,* Jackie Hudson courageously shares, in a personal and stimulating narrative, her own battle to overcome haunting doubts that plagued her for years. She shatters shallow, guilt-producing solutions to this multi-faceted problem. Jackie explores not only the intellectual issues surrounding doubt but the emotional and psychological dimensions as well. I encourage you to read *Doubt: A Road To Growth.* It may save years of unnecessary pain in your growth process to maturity in Christ. You will find this quick, easy-reading book a practical approach to the Christian life, making it a helpful tool for yourself and those you disciple. I highly recommend it to you.

Josh McDowell
Author and Speaker

PREFACE

WHEN YOU MUST

Hurt reaches deep in the soul,
    clutching and tearing
    at all you hold dear.
Pain threatens to destroy
    the dreams you've held
    and truth you've never questioned.

Cry when you must . . .
But cry in His arms.

Fear rises up to conquer
    the certainty of peace
    that has guarded your way.
Thoughts crowd into your mind,
    finding room to dwell
    where you thought none existed.

Doubt when you must . . .
But doubt in His arms.

Hope slips quickly out of reach
    as sand through fingers
    on a hot, sandy beach.
Despair silently, unknowingly
    becomes your companion
    through long, endless days.

11

Give up when you must . . .
But do so in His arms.

Helplessly you rest in your weakness
    until all struggle
    has nowhere to go.
Into His arms you fall;
    having lost all,
    you find Him.

When you must . . .

Jackie Hudson
April 1980

CHAPTER 1

BREAKING OUT OF BOXES

"I'm strong, I'm sure, I'm in control,
a lady with a plan.
Believing that life is a neat little package
I hold in my hand.
I've got it together. They call me the girl
who knows just what to say and do . . ."
Anne Murray[1]

The crowd spilled onto the playing field of the Cotton Bowl in Dallas when 80,000 Christians came to Explo '72. As I watched them, a shattering thought flashed through my mind: *How do all these people really know there is a God?*

I was stunned. *Did I think that? After all, I'm one of the 250 staff members working on this evangelism training conference. We've planned and prayed and worked for months for this. I'm in full-time Christian work! How can I think a thought like that?*

I tried to push the question out of my mind, but

failed. In the weeks that followed, I struggled to keep from drowning in a sea of doubt.

Questions engulfed my mind. *How do I know God exists? Is the Bible really His inspired Word? What about the 2.5 billion people who have never heard about Christ? Are they going to hell? That seems so unfair!*

Sleeping and eating were so difficult for me that I lost nine pounds without trying! Fear, anxiety and panic constantly kept me company. I wanted to believe, but couldn't. No matter how hard I tried, I couldn't stop the doubts.

I confessed them as sin. I memorized Scripture passages. I prayed. I sought help from Christian friends.

But the doubts stubbornly persisted. *Maybe I'm not really a Christian,* I thought. *Maybe I can't believe because I'm not one of the "chosen ones." If I'm not predestined for salvation, I must be going to hell — and I can't do anything about it.*

I had heard that if you are not sure you are a Christian, you should pray one final time and trust Christ to forgive your sins. Then write the date in your bible, and whenever doubts come, look at that date and say, "Christ is in my life as of this date, and I don't have to doubt anymore." Do you know how many dates I had in the front of my Bible? Five.

Most painful was the fact that, with all my heart, I wanted to believe. I remember tears running down my face as I asked my friend Ney Bailey, "What should I do?"

Ney gently put her arm around my shoulders. I felt reassured. My doubts didn't frighten her. "Do you have a minute to talk?" she asked. For the next hour we looked at what the Word had to say about faith and doubt. That was my first step on my journey to understanding the problem.

Doubt rarely jumps out at us from nowhere. Our individual history leads us to those dark periods of lonely questioning. As I reflected on my own temperament and background, I began to understand more clearly my personal encounter with doubt.

In the Beginning

Order. I love order! I've always kept my world incredibly ordered. The idiom, "There's a place for everything and everything has a place," could have originated with me.

And I have a desire for control. For instance, I drove my older brother crazy as I became the maker, keeper, dispenser and controller of the chocolate chip cookies. Once I had memorized the recipe on the back of the Nestle's Toll House Chocolate Chip bag, I made cookies as often as Mom would let me. Now, I realize that half the fun of making cookies is eating the dough. But not in my kitchen! One day my brother swept through the kitchen, grabbing a fingerful of dough on his way. I yelled at the top of my lungs, "Mom, Bill is eating my dough again. Make him quit! He can have some cookies when they're done."

But when the cookies were done, it was just as

difficult to exact a cookie from me, the "keeper of the batch," as it had been to scoop a fingerful of dough. I carefully removed the hot, lightly browned, slightly underdone cookies from the cookie sheet and placed them neatly in groups of twelve on the counter, four across and three deep. I kept an exact count of my cookies, and when I discovered I had an uneven number which messed up my rows, then and only then, did I give my brother a cookie. (I'm surprised I didn't count the number of chocolate chips in each cookie, but who would be *that* fanatical?)

Finally, in utter frustration, my brother screamed, "What are you, the keeper of the bank? Why don't you go rent a vault to store your dumb cookies forever?" After that scene, I finally loosened up, and the cookies disappeared. My desire for control and order had been temporarily satisfied.

Although I've relaxed considerably over the years, my need for order is probably still stronger than the average person's. For example, I like to keep my dresser drawers in perfect order. I prefer to have all my coat hangers hanging in the same direction. I keep my shoes neatly lined up in rows in my closet. I don't leave dirty dishes in the sink. My desk is rarely cluttered. I keep my car cleaned, polished, serviced and full of gas.

The positive impact of my need for order is that often when I am angry or frustrated, I clean! I whip through the house and clean it from top to bottom. It makes me feel so much better. On occasion, Karen, my roommate, has come home from work and commented, "I'm sorry you were frustrated today, but the house looks great. Thanks."

I like living with order. It is my preference.

But there was a time when my preferences were more than just preferences. They were compulsions. It wasn't that I "preferred" to keep a clean house — I "had" to or I could not concentrate on anything else.

But even more serious than how I ordered my external world was my need for control and order in my internal world of feelings, values and faith, and in how I viewed the world. I saw most of life as either black or white, good or bad, right or wrong. Ambiguity was not even in my vocabulary.

Because I was so organized externally and controlled internally, I had an illusion of confidence. I felt I had life figured out, and it fit neatly into my boxes. Everything had a compartment.

Even in my Christian life, I thought I had it all figured out. I trusted Christ as my Savior when I was a nineteen-year-old college sophomore. Because I came from an agnostic background, I experienced quite a change in my life. In fact, I was one of those who are "born running" in their new-found faith. Contentment, peace, joy and genuine enthusiasm characterized my relationship with Jesus Christ. A Christian magazine published an article about me which began: "If Jackie Hudson were to launch her own media campaign, her bumper sticker would read, 'Believe God, and He will do anything.' "

Then somewhere along the way, I fell into my old organize-and-control pattern. I began to categorize my Christian training and principles. Unknowingly, I built boxes for my theology, my faith, and my God.

However, one day my categories and boxes began to crumble. They were too narrow, too rigid. E. Stanley Jones diagnosed my condition when he wrote: "While many people die from hardening of the arteries, others die mentally and spiritually from 'hardening of the categories.' "[2]

For instance, as a young Christian I had learned that early morning was the "biblical time" to spend with God. Jesus was cited as my example (somewhere in the New Testament it says He arose early and went out to pray). Religiously I adhered to this rule, giving God the "best" hour of my day. Before long I squeezed the Lord into His assigned slot every morning.

Then, as my categories softened, I discovered that the Bible also says Jesus prayed all night. In fact, Jesus prayed all the time. That blew my categories apart!

A Universal Problem

Doubt is a common trait. Martin Luther said, "The art of doubting is easy, for it is an ability that is born with us."[3] It comes in all shapes and sizes, and varies from the extreme spiritual doubts which plagued me to simple, everyday doubts such as, Do I want to get up this morning?

It does not matter what your culture is, or your religion. Every human being doubts. In his book In Two Minds Os Guinness suggests that "only God and certain madmen have no doubts."[4]

Because humans are finite and do not possess total knowledge, the door to doubt always stands open. People doubt what they do not understand and question what they do not know.

But what about Christians? Is doubt common to believers also? Yes. Doubt can devastate young believers, and it can render passive the faith of older Christians. We have failed to recognize that doubt is not automatically eliminated from the human condition when we become Christians.

Belief takes time to grow. Often, at the first sign of doubt, young Christians panic, convinced their faith is suddenly deficient. Then faith, or a lack of it, becomes the issue. This supposition that doubt is rooted in our lack of faith can lead to unnecessary guilt and feelings of failure, and the doubter may take erroneous and extreme measures to overcome it.

In fact, Os Guinness plainly states, "The root of doubt is not in our faith but in our humanness."[5]

When I first realized this truth, my response could be summed up in one word — relief! I had given years to introspection regarding my lack of faith. Now, for the first time, I began to join hands with my faith and to tackle my painful doubt problem.

You see, faith was no longer the problem. Faith had moved from the position of "problem" to that of "advocate" to help me overcome the real problem, doubt.

Jesus said, "If you have faith as a mustard seed, you shall say to this mountain, 'Move from here to there,' and it shall move; and nothing shall be impossible to you" (Matthew 17:20). Doubt was my mountain. Looming large in front of me, it threatened to be insurmountable. But with my mustard seed of faith, I began dealing with my doubts — and my faith has grown deeper, richer and more genuine.

After starting my Christian life with incredible energy and faith, I had begun to question the reality of my salvation. Then with what little faith I had at the time, I chose to believe God's Word over my doubts. Christ claimed He would come into my life if I asked Him. Now the responsibility for my assurance was His. Slowly, as I affirmed the truth, my faith grew and my doubts were replaced by the confidence of His presence in my life.

Why a Book on Doubt?

Christians who are struggling with doubt don't talk about it. They are ashamed of it. Or they have resigned themselves to living with it like they would an annoying headache.

Tragically, many Christians today quickly label doubt as "sin" or "unbelief." This adds guilt to the believer's already painful battle, and the condition worsens. For a sensitive "doubter" the struggle can be nearly intolerable. Guinness explains, "What is the most damaging to Christianity is not that Christians doubt, but that there seems to be so little open discussion and understanding of doubt."[6]

The Church, the Body of Christ, should be a place where a believer or sincere skeptic can ask questions and work through doubts safely, no matter how long it takes. If an intelligent person cannot find satisfying answers to his questions within the limits of his finiteness, his faith eventually will erode and become passive — or be destroyed altogether.

I wonder if Bertrand Russell, the famous 20th Century proponent of atheism, would have taken a different road had he found a friendly place to vent his skepticism. Russell believed in God until he was eighteen years old. One reason he stopped believing was the unhealthy attitude he was forced to adopt toward his doubts.[7]

Or consider Carl Rogers, the well-known psychologist. Rogers grew up in a fundamental home, was involved in a Christian organization in college, and studied for the ministry. While living abroad for six months, he observed religious attitudes far different from his own, causing him to question the deity of Jesus. Eventually Rogers parted with his beliefs.[8] Would his life have taken a different turn if he had been able to express his doubts to other Christians and work through those doubts?

During my struggle with doubt, I read everything I could find on the subject. That so few books had been written on doubt disappointed me. But what troubled me more were the shallow solutions given in some of these books as well as the lack of empathy expressed toward the doubter.

One of the most common themes was that doubt is sin, and the doubter should confess it and *decide once and for all* never to doubt again. With my ability to control and organize my life, you would think I could pull off this one simple task, wouldn't you?

But suppressing or denying a problem doesn't work with an inquisitive mind.

People need clarity regarding doubt, as well as encouragement to keep going when they are in the emotional turmoil of facing their questions. If you are in this situation, I want you to know that dealing with doubt can bring you a stronger faith, a more accurate knowledge of God, and a more intimate experience of our Lord's presence in your daily life.

A Road to Growth

As I struggled with doubt, I often wondered, "Has my faith failed?" This was my greatest fear, for if my faith gave way, how could I ever please God, since His Word says, "Without faith it is impossible to please Him"? (Hebrews 11:6)

In the confusion and pain surrounding my doubting, I felt many times that my faith had failed and this devastated me. (How grateful I am that "the LORD is near to the broken hearted, and saves those who are crushed in spirit" (Psalm 34:18). I definitely qualified!)

A number of years ago, the Auca Indians of Eduador speared to death five young missionaries who were attempting to establish communication with them. Elisabeth Elliot, the wife of one of the murdered missionaries, did something that few people would do: She returned to live among the Aucas. Jim, her husband, had died trying to get the message of God's love to these people and Elisabeth continued his work.

For two years she waited, watched, learned the

language, and slowly began interacting with the Auca Indians. It was a time of questioning for her. "My confusion drove me to the admission that I had not as many answers as I had thought."[9]

Elisabeth Elliot's questions and doubts dealt with the integrity and wisdom of superimposing an "American" Christianity upon the Auca culture. Values and ideas she had held about right and wrong, and good and evil, were challenged, and some were changed. She wrote beautifully about the outcome of her search for answers in a book entitled, *The Liberty of Obedience.* The concept of maturity she presented involved not having all the answers, and not knowing all the rules, but rather having our "senses exercised to discern both good and evil" (Hebrews 5:14, KJV).

In light of Elisabeth Elliot's experience in Ecuador, her editor has written about her: "She began to realize that the Christian who has all the answers, the Christian who sees things as all black or all white, just might possibly be the Christian who is so rigid in his commitment that he may never know the liberty of obedience, who is permanently bound to a perpetual immaturity.[10]

Though often I felt my faith had failed, it had not. What had failed were the ordered, rigid, narrow categories I had built around it. Now, I was setting out on my own road of spiritual, personal and emotional growth where a small but vibrant faith could try a few steps and then start to move on toward full maturity. I began breaking out of those boxes. Difficult? Terribly. Slow? Excruciatingly. Worth it?

Absolutely! In some ways, I felt I was starting all over in my walk with God. Maybe I was, but I remember reading that the person who has the courage to go back and make the foundations of his or her faith strong will be the person who pushes through to the end. I wanted to push through to the end.

This book is about doubt, its accompanying pain, and what to do if you are a doubter. But it also talks about growth, for the moment you begin learning how to handle and resolve your doubts, you step onto the road toward growth.

My prayer is that the answers I have found and the lessons I have learned will help you face the difficult obstacles of doubt in your Christian life.

CHAPTER 2

THE DOUBTER'S DILEMMA

"I do believe; help me in my unbelief."
Mark 9:24

Hello!" the hazy, faraway sound told me immediately it was a long-distance call.

"Jackie Hudson?"

"Yes."

"Ney Bailey suggested I call you," a man's voice said. Ney is the author of the book *Faith Is Not A Feeling*. "I read in her book about your struggle with doubt, and I called her. She referred me to you. I am experiencing the same thing you were. I want to believe, but I can't! No matter what I try, I'm unable to stop the doubts. I am preoccupied with them. This whole thing is affecting my work and my family. I feel trapped and that scares me!" His voice sounded frantic.

"I know I need more faith," he continued, "but I can't seem to believe enough to stop the doubts. Do you have time to talk?"

Memories and feelings flooded back as I listened for the next hour. *Lord, help me know what to say,* I silently prayed. *I feel his agony, I know his desperation.* I could sense the pain, the pain that always seems to accompany doubt. I could hear how it was paralyzing this man. In his unique way, he expressed the dilemma common to all those who wander in a maze of doubt: "I want to believe, but I don't seem to have enough faith."

The doubter is caught in a bind. He thinks he lacks faith, yet the prerequisite for eliminating his doubt is faith. He can't trust, but the only way to resolve his doubt is to trust. He can't believe, but the only thing able to conquer his unbelief is belief.

This never-ending paradox renders the doubter helpless. He feels doomed to a life of doubt, trapped by his own inadequacy and unable to reverse his emotional downward spiral. At times he feels angry at the situation, at God, or at himself. At other times, he simply feels defeated and passive.

Let me assure you that doubt does not have to immobilize anyone. No one needs to remain its victim. The issue is complex, but I have found extremely helpful insights — perspectives that resolve multitudes of questions. These truths can help you, too.

You may be crying out for one profound answer that will resolve, once and for all, the whole mess, but it usually doesn't happen that way. I had to unravel my dilemma by pulling out many strings, one after another, one at a time, until I finally found intellectual and emotional clarity. Then doubt lost its power over me. There was no one answer — over the years I have discovered many truths which, when synthesized, ultimately have unraveled the knots and freed me from bondage to doubt.

You have to begin somewhere. I found my starting point by pursuing one thought. I began by seeking an understanding of what the Bible says about doubt, and about faith.

Understanding Doubt

What is doubt? How you answer this question is critical, for it will determine how you deal with doubt. Is it the same as unbelief? Is it the opposite of faith? Is it sin?

For years, I assumed doubt was synonymous with unbelief, and therefore, it was sin. I held the view that for my faith to be genuine, it must be doubt-free. I put doubt in almost the same camp as the "unpardonable sin." So negative was my view that I unknowingly attached a negative moral value to doubt. If I doubted, I was bad. Only sub-standard Christians had doubts.

These views sustained me for a while. As long as I didn't have doubts, I was OK. If they were minimal, then I could categorize them as sin, confess them, move on and still feel good about myself. But when the lid came off and my doubts became obsessive, those same views became my enemies.

My faith must not be genuine, I thought. *Maybe I've really committed the unpardonable sin!* I began to feel bad about myself. It took me years to see the fallibility of my perspective and to replace it with an accurate one.

Doubt has different degrees and is used in various ways in the Bible. I was comforted to learn that in the New Testament "doubt is an affair of the believer rather than the unbeliever."[1] It is rare to find a Christian who has not doubted at some point.

A number of New Testament words translate into English as doubt. Although varying to some degree, these words are similar in their emphasis on ambivalence or double-mindedness.[2] The English word *doubt* comes from Latin and means "two."[3] Putting these together, Os Guinness states, "To believe is to be in 'one mind' about accepting something as true; to disbelieve is to be in 'one mind' about rejecting it. To doubt is to waiver between the two, to believe and disbelieve at once, and so to be 'in two minds.' "[4] He goes on to say, "The heart of doubt is a divided heart."[5]

What is doubt, then? It is that state of being suspended between faith and unbelief.[6] It is a mind that is undecided, pulled between two options. Doubt, you might say, is a "half-way stage."[7] Looking closely at James 1:6-8, we find this example:

> For the one who doubts is like the surf of
> the sea driven and tossed by the wind. For let
> not that man expect that he will receive anything
> from the Lord, being a double-minded man,
> unstable in all his ways.

James uses a vivid mental picture to describe this uncertain condition. Anyone who has ever been in this position is painfully aware of the resulting agony. Have you ever watched the turmoil a young man experiences when he is hopelessly in love, but can't make up his mind whether to marry or not? He's like a wave tossed by the wind, surging back and forth in his indecision. James describes this ambivalent state so well that I wonder if he went through a time of doubt. The term, double-minded, which he uses to describe the man of doubt, does not appear in secular literature or in the Scriptures until James uses it here in verse 8. It is defined as "two-souled."[8]

Biblical scholar James Ropes argues that this man's soul is divided between the world and faith in God.[9] Bunyan epitomized the idea with his character, Mr. Facing-Both-Ways.[10] Augustine's prayer captured the thought as he said, "Oh, Lord, grant me purity, but not yet."[11] The final result, as the Bible says, is that this man is unstable in all his ways. This insecurity characterizes his entire life. The condition is one of painful, chronic instability.

Therefore, doubt is not the opposite of faith. The New Testament distinction between unbelief and doubt is clear. Os Guinness says, "The word *unbelief* is usually used as a willful refusal to believe, or of a deliberate decision to disobey. It is the consequence of a settled choice. Since it is a deliberate response to God's truth, unbelief is definitely held to be responsible."[12] The New Testament warns against the danger of unbelief. Unbelief *is* the opposite of faith.

Jesus did not respond to unbelief.[13] But He seemed always to have time for a sincere doubter or questioner. Even when the father of a demonic boy labeled his own doubt as unbelief, Jesus responded by healing the man's son.[14] He may have responded differently had the man's doubt been unbelief.

When I realized that doubt was not the same as unbelief, and therefore not condemned by Jesus or by the New Testament, I began to relax. My horrible stabs of guilt had been primarily self-induced. I had been condemning myself when the Bible was giving me grace and room to grow. I began to see Jesus on my side, helping me overcome my doubts rather than judging me for my "unbelief."

Yet I still had another question. Doubt is not the sin of unbelief, but is it sin? Fortunately, the Bible does not clearly answer this question. Otherwise, at the first sign of doubt, we could easily fall into the trap of labeling ourselves and others as having sinned.

When doubt is addressed in the New Testament, the focus is not on sin. Instead it is on the nature of doubt and on moving from doubt to faith. So to determine when it is sin, we need to look at the context of each situation.

The doubt in James 1:6-8 apparently is sin because, in the face of God's explicit promise, the man seems *unwilling* to trust. It appears to be an issue of allegiance to either God or the world. This man isn't struggling with doubt while *wanting* to believe; rather, it appears he isn't sure if he wants *to* believe or *not to* believe.

The father of the demonic boy referred to earlier longed for his son to be healed, but he wasn't sure Jesus could do it. He expressed doubt. After Jesus gave him a brief lesson on the power of believing, the man cried out, "I do believe; help me in my unbelief!"[15] He desperately *wanted* to believe, but still found himself doubting. Without condemnation or mention of sin, Jesus stepped in and met the man's need. Apparently that man's doubt was not sin.

Doubt is sin when it rejects the evidence God has given.[16] (However, we must be careful in judging this in another person, because only God really knows a person's heart.) It is not sin when a person is honestly questioning or needs more information upon which to base his faith.

Doubt is not always sin, but it is always serious. We need to avoid the extremes of overemphasizing the sinfulness of doubt and of downplaying its seriousness. The key is a balanced biblical perspective.

Gaining a biblical perspective was my first step in experiencing freedom from doubt. As I studied the New Testament, I saw little condemnation surrounding doubt and much encouragement to move from a stage of doubt toward faith. This freed me to look at my doubts and resolve them, rather than simply confess them as sin and try to ignore them.

I realized that my doubting did not mean I had no faith. In fact, the reverse was true. Because I believed something in the first place, I had something to doubt. I had faith, but my faith was hurting. It was undernourished, confused, unhealthy. It needed immediate attention so that instead of moving toward unbelief it would move toward full belief.

Understanding doubt did not give me a license to doubt; instead, it gave me freedom to believe.

Understanding Faith

The Bible is filled with stories about the defeats and triumphs of people of faith. It is a book about believing. Since doubt is faith in trouble, let's take a brief glance at what the Bible says about faith.

Scripture defines it as "the assurance of things hoped for, the conviction of things not seen" (Hebrews 11:1). Faith is a belief that what God *says* is true and that what He *says will happen* is a certainty.

The most important lesson I learned about faith began the day I cried out to my friend, "Ney, I can't believe. What should I do?"

Tenderly, she led me through the pages of Scripture and explained faith to me. "Jackie, faith is simply taking God at His Word. In Luke 7 a centurion said to Jesus, *'Just say the word,* and my servant will be healed' (verse 7). The Lord was amazed at this man's great faith."

Ney paused and looked at me. "So you see, faith is taking God at His Word. You can substitute this phrase whenever the Bible uses faith."

That was the most practical definition of faith I had ever heard. It became even more clear as Ney took me to the book of Hebrews and began reading, "By faith Noah, being warned by God about things not yet seen, in reverence prepared an ark" (Hebrews 11:7).

"Jackie, what did God tell Noah to do?" Ney asked.

"Build an ark," I replied.

"What did Noah do?"

"He built an ark."

"So you see, Noah 'took God at His Word' and built an ark," Ney said. "Let's read that verse again, this way: Taking God at His Word, Noah prepared an ark."

I got the point. Faith went from being mystical, and hard to grasp, to being very practical. "Taking God at His Word" became a working definition of faith, not just a theological definition.

As time went on, I learned other important lessons regarding faith. In the midst of my doubts, I had been troubled by the question: What if God hasn't chosen to give me faith, and that's why I can't believe? I now strongly believe that all of Scripture affirms that if a person *wants* to believe, God will give him faith. There is no biblical evidence of a person sincerely seeking the Lord ever being turned away or refused faith. God desires that the world come to Him. He would never withhold the one necessary ingredient. If a person *wants* to have faith and is deeply troubled because he is afraid he doesn't have it, that is excellent evidence that, *indeed,* he does have faith. Thus, it is more productive for that person to turn his attention from whether or not he has faith toward what is troubling his faith. Where does his faith need attention?

Another lesson involved feelings, with which I subtly had measured my faith. When I *felt* I had faith, I was on top of the world. When I *didn't feel* I had faith, I was devastated. I slowly began to see that even when I didn't feel I had faith, I really did, and I could choose with my will to take God at His Word. Faith, in essence, is a choice.

I purposely began to establish a habit of believing by taking God at His Word, whether or not I felt I had any faith. The process took time and patience.

For example, I never considered myself a valuable person while growing up. I didn't think I mattered much. But in reading the Bible I saw that God said something very different about me. He said I did matter! I was so valuable that Christ died for me. I now had a choice: I could take God at His Word and believe I was valuable, or I could continue to believe my feelings. I chose to believe Him. Changing deep-rooted feelings took time. But I had established a new habit.

Finally, I began to learn that faith had more to do with God than with me. Not only is Jesus the "author and perfecter of faith" (Hebrews 12:2), but He also is the object of our faith. He gives us faith that we might depend on Him. And as we depend on Him, our faith grows. Biblical faith is trust in a person — Jesus Christ. When I began to look less at whether I had any faith and more at the character of the one I was trusting, my doubts began to lose their power.

Learning that faith was taking God at His Word, that it was a choice, and that it has more to do with God than it has to do with me, put me on the road to a stronger, healthier faith.

Putting It All Together

Gaining a biblical understanding of doubt and of faith began to solve what had seemed an impossible dilemma. Before, I wandered in darkness, bumping into and stumbling over my questions and doubts. I felt helpless, hopeless, spiritually and emotionally defeated. This scriptural insight, however, shed a small ray of light in the darkness. When I saw I wasn't trapped and helpless, my hope slowly began to return.

Here's how it looked when I began putting it all together. I realized that my doubt was not unbelief; it was faith caught between believing and not believing. I had at least a mustard seed of faith! And with that seed, I could choose to take God at His Word. As I chose to take God at His Word, I began to see more clearly the loving character of the one I desired to trust. When I saw His character, I realized He wasn't condemning me for my doubt. I also saw that much of my doubt had not been sin.

This realization reduced the paralyzing effect of guilt. And it freed me to begin seeing God in the midst of my doubts. I began to see, while still doubting, that God was the protector of my faith. That gave me the courage to keep facing and working through my doubts.

A Place to Start

The following are some beginning steps you can take even during the times of most intense doubt.

1. *Recognize that faith and doubt can co-exist.* This eliminates the pressure of thinking that for your faith to be genuine it must be doubt-free. Until we meet the Lord one day, our faith will never be totally free of doubt, because it's not yet perfect. A healthy faith, however, will be free from nagging, paralyzing doubt.

2. *Be brutally honest with God about your doubts.* God is big enough and strong enough to handle all your questions and doubts, although He may not answer every one. No question you can throw at Him will catch Him off-guard. The Bible tells us that "all the treasures of wisdom and knowledge" are hidden in Christ (Colossians 2:3). By being honest with God, we guard against an unhealthy repression of our emotional turmoil.

3. *Practice taking God at His Word.* Acknowledge, accept and explore your doubts and the accompanying painful feelings. Your prayer might sound something like this:

"Lord, I'm doubting whether I'm a Christian. That terrifies me. Your Word says, 'But as many as received Him, to them He gave the right to become children of God' (John 1:12). I know I've received You. I choose to take You at Your Word that I'm Your child, but Lord, I'm still afraid. Would You show me where my doubt is coming from? Help me to sort through this issue."

Remember that your confusion and emotional turmoil may not change overnight. Resolving the problem of doubt is a process. But in the meantime, you need not remain doubt's victim.

These beginning steps were crucial to my progress in overcoming doubt. I still had battles to fight, however, for it seemed no matter how hard I tried, my doubts were persistent. They just wouldn't go away . . .

CHAPTER 3

THE ORIGIN OF DOUBT

*"The root of doubt is not in our faith
but in our humanness."*

Os Guinness[1]

*Why are my doubts so persistent? I wondered.
Why can't I just decide, "once and for all," never
to doubt again? Life would be so much easier.*

My obsessive doubts drove me to find answers.
I read anything and everything that even remotely
related to my questions. At any given time, someone
could come into my room and find me buried under
a stack of books. In one hand, I'd be holding a book
by C. S. Lewis; in the other, one by Francis Schaeffer.
A third book would lie open on the floor in front
of me. Several others, partially read, would be scat-
tered around me.

As a result of my studying I could answer questions most Christians never even ask. I knew all sides of most major theological issues. I had devoured the historical evidence surrounding Christianity. I probably could have persuaded an atheist it was not only reasonable but also just plain smart to believe in God.

Yet, in spite of all this knowledge, I could not stop my own doubts. I wondered why.

I was looking in the wrong place! I failed to see, as Os Guinness says, that "while God is the answer to all doubt, theologically correct God-answers are not necessarily the answer . . . there are also spiritual, moral, and especially psychological dimensions to doubt."[2]

I had nearly completed work for a graduate degree in theology. My friends will attest to the fact that I also had become the foremost Christian apologist of our three-person household! Yet all the studying in the world wouldn't stop my doubts, because my problem wasn't theological or intellectual. I swallowed my pride and dared to question, Could my problem be psychological?

I discovered the answer to that question and the missing link to my struggle as I explored the question, Where does doubt come from?

And Great Was Their Fall

Doubt has its root in the fall of man. Before Adam and Eve sinned, they enjoyed perfect fellowship with God. According to Dr. Cyril Barber and Dr.

Gary Strauss in their book *Leadership: The Dynamics of Success,* in the Garden of Eden the first couple's basic needs were met: the need to feel a sense of belonging, of worth and of competence.[3] Not only were their needs met, but also the different aspects of their personalities (the mind, the emotions and the will) were in complete harmony. God was the center of their lives. They were secure.

Psychologists call this "congruence." In his epistle, James refers to it as being complete. The concept James portrays is one of wholeness and perfection, with nothing lacking.[4]

In the garden, Adam and Eve had no knowledge of "double-mindedness." It was outside their experience to doubt, because their personalities were whole. Faced with a choice, though, the couple disobeyed God. This event is referred to as the Fall. The effect of the Fall was monumental! As Barber and Strauss explain, "They passed from total security to a gnawing, anxious insecurity in a few moments' time."[5] Adam and Eve severed their relationship with God, cutting off their source of spiritual life. They lost their sense of belonging, worth and competence. Before, God had been the central point of their lives. Now "self" stood at the center. They no longer depended on God as the source of human dignity, but rather turned to themselves to find their identity. In essence, self replaced God; insecurity replaced security; anxiety replaced congruence. And ever since, man has lived in a perpetual state of instability. *This is the root of human doubt.*

Os Guinness explains that doubt is human, it is universal, and it originated at the Fall.[6]

When a person places his trust in Christ, his relationship with God is restored. Yet, although he has experienced redemption, the believer lives with tension in his life because of his old nature. He still feels the effects of the Fall.

So What?

Christian maturity is a process. And in this process God works through the normal development of human personality as the Holy Spirit empowers the believer.[7] The influence of parenting and the environment a person grows up in is central to the development of the personality. I am not a theologian or a psychologist, but to my understanding as a layperson, people need to have a sense of their own identity; to feel good about who they are and what they can do. This is what I would call having a healthy sense of "self."

Stated simplistically, from the time we are young, as we interact with our parents and eventually our friends, as we engage in the tasks around us, and as we learn about God, we either internalize a *good* sense of self from numerous positive encounters, or we internalize a *bad* sense of self from numerous negative encounters.

To the degree that a person lacks this positive realization internally, he is in need of emotional growth. Since no one had perfect parenting, and because of the Fall, we all have that need.

Therefore, as a result of immaturity in one area of our personality, it is possible to find ourselves in a state of doubt.[8]

My own life is a good example. I remember sitting across the table from Ney at Marie Callender's, a favorite restaurant. I will never forget looking her straight in the eyes and nearly choking over the words that came out of my mouth.

"Ney, I've tried everything I know to do, and I can't stop doubting. I think . . . what I mean is, Ney, I think I need professional help."

I began to cry. I felt humiliated. After all, I had been in full-time Christian work for eight years. What would people think of me if they knew I was getting counseling? But, at that moment, I didn't care. Pride or no pride, I needed help to solve the problem of doubt in my life. My relationship with the Lord meant too much to me to let my doubting go on any longer.

As if she had been reading my mind, Ney said, "Jackie, it takes courage to step out and get help. I really respect you for that."

I needed to hear that.

She continued, "I believe that once you've done everything you know to do, once you've exhausted all your resources, if the problem still persists, then it just may have an emotional root. I think that's why God has given us good Christian counselors and psychologists. I'll go with you, if you'd like." Ney accompanied me that very day to see a counselor.

I pray that I never again have to go through

the dark, lonely times that followed. Painful memories and feelings were buried deep inside me. Those feelings screamed at me that no one could be trusted. They cried at the very core of my being that if I trust, I will be treated in a cruel manner. I will be humiliated.

With my mind I was affirming God's trustworthiness in light of His revealed Word and character. But my unconscious feelings won the battle. My emotions had greater influence over my will than did my intellect, and I doubted. I was plunged into a sea of agonizing "double-mindedness."

Why were my doubts so persistent? Why couldn't I just decide "once and for all" never to doubt again? Through counseling I discovered it was because my doubts were not intellectually based. Rather, they were emotionally based. Trust is the key element in the Christian life and I needed help trusting.

Early in my Christian life, I chose with my will to trust the Lord. As long as I kept my emotions highly controlled, I was fine. But when my emotions refused to be held down any longer, the feeling that it was not safe to trust attached itself to the one person I was dependent upon: God. I felt an unconscious terror at being dependent on someone who would hurt me or treat me cruelly, and my only defense was to doubt.

It wasn't until I began the process of healing for those painful memories and damaged emotions that I could differentiate my past feelings from the present reality. In my past, it hadn't been safe to trust. But I learned that today, especially in light of the trustworthy character of God, it not only was safe to trust as an act of my will, but it was also safe to trust with the full weight of my emotions.

Slowly my doubts faded. It was difficult, but well worth it. Did I ever want to give up? All the time! But I didn't. Today I'm not only free from the obsessive doubting, but I am growing in every area of my life.

The Process of Growth

Growth is difficult. It inevitably involves tension between your old nature and your new nature.[9] It also involves time to correct your faulty thinking as more truth is discovered. There will not always be congruence in your personality,[10] and at times you will experience ambivalent feelings, insecurity, and confusion, and, perhaps make wrong choices. These were a part of my daily experience as I grew in overcoming my doubts.

For example, one morning I awoke startled. Terror gripped me and doubts bombarded my mind. *Where am I? What time is it?* I panicked in the darkness and grabbed my clock. It was four o'clock. Then I remembered I'd had great difficulty getting to sleep the night before. And it had been only a few hours! "Please, God, let me sleep. Please! My only escape from these doubts is sleep. I'm so scared," I cried.

I got out of bed and tip-toed into my roommate's bedroom.

"Karen, it's me. I'm afraid, and I can't sleep,"

I whispered. This was not the first time. Karen moved her legs and made room for me to curl up at the bottom of her twin bed. (Now, that's a friend!)

"It's okay. Sleep here," she whispered back. I still don't know why we whispered. Within seconds she was fast asleep again. (I hate people who have no trouble sleeping.) I pulled my comforter over me as I curled up next to her legs where it was warm. It helped me not to feel so all alone. Finally, I slept.

This conflict does not equal a lack of trust. It is not necessarily sin. When you turn from trusting God to trusting yourself, you have sinned, but how often has the legitimate growth process of the believer been labeled "sin," adding guilt to an already difficult process?

If your doubts are emotionally based like mine were, give yourself time. Let God restore your ability to make right choices. Be patient with yourself as He heals your damaged emotions and corrects your faulty thinking. In becoming a Christian, you went through a radical change. The very center of your life was changed from being self-oriented to being God-oriented. This restoration was instantaneous, yet a lifetime process is involved if you are to see the results in every area of your personality.

I found the missing link to my doubts. However, the principle I had clung to through most of my doubting days was still to be discovered. How do you live in an ambiguous world where doubt is never far away?

CHAPTER 4

LIFE IN THE GRAY ZONE

"The world of Christian faith is not a fairy-tale,
make-believe world, question-free
and problem-proof, but a world
where doubt is never far from faith's shoulder."
                    Os Guinness[1]

Have you ever thought about how much of life is lived in "the gray zone" — that ambiguous state between black and white, good and bad, right and wrong?

I spent years living in the "black and white zone." I believed there was a right way to do things, and a wrong way. It never crossed my mind that there might be two equally effective methods for accomplishing the same task. Experiences were either all good or all bad. People were either all good or all bad. Every choice I made was either right or wrong.

I lived in extremes. I either loved something or hated it. This mentality demanded certainty and absolutes. It made life simple, boring and extremely unrealistic.

But time and experience have a way of forcing us to be realistic. That is what happened to me. As I encountered the complexities of life, I eventually had to face the reality that rarely is anything absolutely black or white. Usually it is gray.[2]

Every day we face questions that don't have simple answers. How many times have we cried out, "Lord, I prayed for guidance. *Why* is everything falling apart? *How long* is this difficult situation going to last? *Why* do You allow suffering and evil, God?"

It is precisely here that doubt, if not handled maturely, can take its toll on faith. We face the challenge of balancing faith with the ambiguity that difficult questions raise. The key to that balance is practicing the principle of suspended judgment.

Learning to Suspend Judgment

What does it mean to suspend judgment? I learned about this principle while reading *In Two Minds* by Os Guinness. He clarifies the concept in his chapter titled "Keyhole Theology."

Inherent in the idea of suspended judgment are two elements.

First, a believer must have sufficient reason for trusting God in the first place. Knowing why he trusts God will allow the believer to trust God when he can't understand what He is doing. "The truth is this: We can always have sure and sufficient reasons for knowing why we can trust God, but we cannot always know what God is doing, and why."[3]

Second, to suspend judgment does not mean we cease to use our minds. It does not mean we stop asking questions. God has given us minds with which to think, explore and reason. Suspending judgment *does* mean that we put reason in its place by stopping short of making a judgment about God when we don't understand what He is doing.

To suspend judgment, then, is not irrational. It simply means that we have sufficient reason to keep trusting, based on truth and experience, even when we don't understand. To suspend judgment allows God to be God and allows our faith to take us beyond the finite boundaries of our reason. "As believers, we cannot always know why, but we can always know why we trust God who knows why, and that makes all the difference," states Guinness.[4]

John the Baptist is an example of someone who doubted, but who seemed to practice the principle of suspended judgment.

You may ask, "John the Baptist, a doubter?"

Here was the man of whom Jesus Himself said, "Among those born of women, there has not arisen anyone greater than John the Baptist" (Matthew 11:11).

Here was the man who was prophesied about in the Old Testament as the one who would prepare the way for the coming of the Lord.[5]

Here was the man who summed up all of Jewish hope and history in one statement when he saw Jesus and exclaimed, "Behold, the Lamb of God who takes away the sin of the world!" (John 1:29)

Here was the man who baptized the Lord. Yet John the Baptist expressed doubt.

John's Experience

The scene opens with John having been thrown into prison for the terrible crime of confronting Herod on a moral issue.[6] How long he had been in prison we don't know. I imagine John was dirty and hungry. Darkness surrounded him day and night. Perhaps he was tired and discouraged. In this filthy, lonely prison cell, John began hearing about the amazing works Jesus was performing. So he sent his followers to Jesus with one urgent question: "Are You the coming one, or shall we look for someone else?" (Matthew 11:3)

Exactly why John was doubting or questioning is somewhat unclear in the passage. It appears, however, that his questions had something to do with who Jesus was or what Jesus was doing. We know this, because one aspect of the Lord's reply to John was, "Blessed is he who keeps from stumbling over *Me*" (Matthew 11:6).

In his confusion, John could have said, "Jesus, You are not doing what I think You are supposed to be doing. Maybe I should quit believing in You."

But right here, I believe, is where John suspended judgment. He refused to make a judgment about Jesus, or what He was doing, based on limited information. Instead, he went right to the source with his question. Then he waited and trusted.

I love the Lord's response to John's messengers: "Go and report to John the things which you hear and see: the blind receive sight and the lame walk, the lepers are cleansed and the deaf hear, and the dead are raised up, and the poor have the gospel preached to them" (Matthew 11:4,5).

Jesus quoted the prophet Isaiah. He took John back to the Word of God. I have a hunch Jesus knew that John would recognize that prophetic passage about the coming Messiah. John was a man steeped in the knowledge of the Old Testament. In recognizing the passage, John could not help but put two and two together. He may well have thought, *This Jesus is doing exactly what the prophet Isaiah said He would do. He is the coming one, and I need not look for someone else.*

John dealt with his doubts by refusing to judge what Jesus was doing based on limited information. Instead, in the midst of his doubts, he waited and trusted. This, then, is what it means to suspend judgment.

Help, I Need Guidance!

"My doubts are not extreme. They often are trivial. When something goes wrong, I turn to God for guidance. Sometimes He is silent. That's when I find myself doubting His care."

"I don't doubt the existence of God or the

validity of the Scriptures. But sometimes I feel at
the end of my rope. I can't handle it any more.
That's when I doubt God's guidance — or lack of it."

"I was certain God was leading me to ask her
to marry me. I was so sure, but she refused me.
Did God trick me? How could I have totally missed
His direction?"

Inevitably, when I speak on doubt, I am confronted with statements like these. What do you do
when you think God was leading you but the results
are not what you planned? What do you do when
you seek the Lord but are faced with an absence of
guidance? It is easy to *say*, "God, I don't understand
Your silence right now, but I know why I trust You.
Therefore, I will suspend judgment. I will wait."

But, as with most things, that is easier said
than done. We would like to tell our friends what
John the Baptist said: "Go ask Jesus and come right
back to tell me *immediately.*"

When the pressure mounts, so do the questions.
"God, why are You silent?" "Have You forgotten
Your promise to guide me?" "Did I do something
wrong?" "Am I on the wrong road?" "Don't You care
anymore?" "Maybe I've been fooling myself and
none of this faith stuff is real." Os Guinness says,
"Faith tosses and turns like a man delirious in fever."[7]

The questions become emphatic. We demand an
answer *now.*

At times like these, it is easy to forget what
God has done in the past. In fact, the past can
become nonexistent. The many times in which God

has answered prayer and intimately guided us become cloudy. We easily forget God's good intentions toward us as promised in His Word . . . "For I know the plans that I have for you . . . plans for welfare and not for calamity to give you a future and a hope" (Jeremiah 29:11).

When the present darkness becomes the believer's only reality, it is crucial to focus on *remembering*. It may help to take a piece of paper, find a quiet, familiar place, and begin writing down all the times you can remember from the past when God has guided you. Think about the many times He tenderly and faithfully led you through the darkness. Slowly, your faith will find a renewed sense of courage.

Remember, also, that it is OK to ask questions. The Lord even encourages it when He says, "Come now, and let us reason together" (Isaiah 1:18). But be cautioned not to cross that fine line between asking and accusing. To *ask* opens communication. To *accuse* makes the accused our enemy and destroys communication. Suspending judgment of God isn't always easy, but it is the only way to maintain the integrity of our faith, and at the same time, to not repress or deny our painful situation.

The challenge for our faith, then, is to say, "God, I am in the dark about guidance, but I am not in the dark about You."[8] Even St. Augustine said, "You were guiding me as a helmsman steers a ship, but the course You steered was beyond my understanding."[9]

How Long, Oh Lord?

Waiting is arduous. My own response to waiting ranges from mild to acute frustration. I can feel angry, humiliated, let down, discouraged, or helpless. Waiting is one of the most difficult tasks we face in life. And in the long, endless hours, months, and many times years of waiting, doubts can flourish.

I was encouraged when I read in the Scriptures that Moses struggled with waiting. He learned his lesson about impatience the hard way — through failure. In his impatience to see the children of Israel freed from their bondage to Egypt, Moses killed an Egyptian. In fear, he fled to the wilderness and stayed there forty years, until it was God's time to free His people.[10]

Abraham blew it, too. God promised him and Sarah a child, even in their old age. But Abraham couldn't wait for God's timing. Instead, he took Hagar, Sarah's maid, to himself and had Ishmael.[11] This was *not* the child God had promised.

In times of waiting, believers face two temptations. One is to take matters into their own hands, as Moses and Abraham did. The other is to passively resign themselves altogether and give up.

But when we suspend judgment in the face of waiting, we choose neither of these options. We don't hurry God's promise or doubt His timing by taking matters into our own hands. Nor do we doubt that God will ever appear on the scene, and thus give up. Rather, we wait and keep working. We stay involved in what we are doing, and we trust. This is a basic skill of faith.[12]

Knowing this does not diminish the difficulty of waiting. For in times of waiting, it is so easy to feel that life is passing you by. It can be incredibly demoralizing. It hurts to see your friends and colleagues moving ahead in life, motivated and eager. You are likely to feel "put on a shelf," a "has-been." Loneliness can become a constant companion. And it becomes difficult to suspend judgment.

Waiting also produces a tension, which can make it even more difficult. Yet tension is a part of our faith. The root meaning of *faith* in the Hebrew implies tautness or tension.[13] This tension exists because, as believers, we live much of the time in that space between God's promise and God's fulfillment.[14]

Guinness explains that "faith's task is to join hands with the past and the future to hold down God's will in the present."[15] I believe this is what Noah did when God spoke to him of the coming flood. With one hand, Noah held on to God's past promise — that there would be a flood. He then reached out with his other hand and grasped tightly to the future fulfillment of the promise — that the rains would indeed come. In the present, he built an ark.[16]

In other words, Noah waited and worked. I don't think it was easy. Years passed between the promise and the fulfillment. Noah's neighbors must have doubted his sanity as he built an ark on dry land — land that never had seen rain. He was alone in a world that thought differently than he did. He lived in the tension between the promise and the fulfillment — and that is faith.

In Hebrews 11, faith's "Hall of Fame," you will find similar examples. Consider Abraham, Moses, Sarah, Joseph and all the others. They lived in that span between God's promise and His fulfillment. Sometimes they failed. They became discouraged. They doubted. But they held tightly to God's promise. They kept going. And in the end, what a tribute they received. "Therefore God is not ashamed to be called their God" (Hebrews 11:16).

Waiting is a lonely, painful business. At times your faith will feel stretched to the breaking point as it is pulled taut between God's promise and His fulfillment. Doubt will come, but you can overcome it by suspending judgment and working. It is a process. Be patient with yourself. And remember the Lord's words to Habakkuk: "Though it tarries [the fulfillment of the promise], wait for it; for it will certainly come, it will not delay" (Habakkuk 2:3).

No Pat Answers

Suspending judgment can be very helpful in handling valid intellectual questions which are particularly stretching for our faith — questions such as, Why does God allow suffering and evil? If God is good and does nothing about suffering, does that mean He is impotent? If He is sovereign and chooses not to stop evil, is He sadistic? Since God is the creator of all things, is He the author of evil? Does mankind really have "free choice"? Are we predestined to heaven or hell?

Questions such as these are difficult, to put it

mildly. There are no pat answers.

Yet, I once thought there were. Until I felt the pain of my own doubts, these questions fit neatly into my rigid system. I tucked them away in their assigned compartments.

I think I even felt superior to people who struggled with such questions. I would respond, "Look, if you will choose to believe God, the feelings these questions have provoked will go away. It is up to you; be strong, control your feelings."

For a time, this approach worked for me. Then my personal pain infused these questions with intrusive force. Before, they seemed remote, lifeless, unimportant. But suddenly they bombarded my mind, tore at my heart and left me feeling crushed and impotent.

Why did these questions become so devastating? Because my system demanded an air-tight explanation, and I found none. My system pushed for structure; I found ambiguity. My system called for continuity; I found paradox. My system required clarity; I found mystery.

Have you ever tried to grab hold of a mystery? Have you ever tried to find security in elusiveness? You want to settle an issue once and for all, but like so many issues, it inherently demands open-mindedness, flexibility and progressive insight — not once-and-for-all closure.

In grappling with difficult questions, I felt like a child who, in his haste to climb a tree, grabs a branch, fully expecting it to hold his weight. Instead the branch is brittle and dead, lacking strength and flexibility. It snaps. The sensation is awful. The child feels panicked, out of control, helpless, terrified. The falling sensation leaves him nauseated. Gratefully, it lasts only seconds, and he lands startled, yet unhurt, on the ground.

I experienced that sensation as I tried to make sense out of these questions. But it lasted more than seconds. The feeling became my unwelcome companion from the moment I woke up in the morning until I fell asleep again at night.

Finding answers was no easy task. More difficult, though, was learning to live with the answers I found. They were sufficient but somewhat ambiguous, since these questions extend beyond the realm of the finite. These questions pierce into the infinite, so only God can make ultimate sense of them. That is precisely why it is so crucial for us to suspend judgment.

If a person has sufficient reason to trust God in the first place, then he will be able to trust God with the inexplicable. Guinness says, "To put it another way, the rationality of faith is implacably opposed to absurdity, but has no quarrel with mystery; it can tell the difference between the two."[17]

In my personal search for answers, I made the following observations:

1. Personal, emotional pain infuses these otherwise academic theological questions with urgency and power.

2. Quick, easy answers are as cruel as they are

inadequate. These questions all have one thing in common: Their answers lie outside the realm of our finite minds. At best, we can only speculate and formulate theories.

3. These questions all tear at the heart of two basic Christian doctrines: the goodness of God and the sovereignty of God. To suspend judgment means holding these two truths in balance. Both are true regardless of the seeming contradiction of the question or situation.

What is easy to state in theory is much more difficult to apply in reality. Learning to suspend judgment in the face of these questions takes practice. It also requires support and care from people who love you. Don't go it alone.

Why I was allowed in the hospital room those few days before Mr. Williams died, I don't remember. Debbie was my roommate and I knew her family, but not intimately enough to join in those sacred moments loved ones share when together they face the stark reality of death.

Six months earlier, Debbie's father was diagnosed as having leukemia. Now the family members stood around his bed, trying to soak in those remaining moments of his life. Their lives had changed dramatically in six short months. Now they seemed to have reconciled themselves to his imminent death.

I stood in the background, feeling awkward, uncomfortable, saying nothing. Debbie just wanted me to be there. Sometimes family members cried;

at other times they even laughed. Then an awkward silence would permeate the room until someone hesitantly spoke again. I remember feeling numb.

I would have done anything to help. I did what I could. I worked hard — I cleaned their house, helped operate their restaurant, ran errands. But to just *be* there with them was so hard. I didn't know what to *do;* I didn't know what to *say.* I longed to find words that would ease the pain of loss and the ugliness of death. I said nothing.

Why does God allow suffering and evil? Why do good people suffer? I had memorized answers to these questions as a part of my training to be a campus missionary. I was well equipped to answer college students, who frequently used these questions as smokescreens to the real issue of man's need for salvation. But now my rote responses seemed shallow, almost cruel.

Theologically and philosophically, the answers I had learned were adequate, but they were inappropriate in this situation. They even failed to comfort me as I silently watched the Williams family struggle with the emotional realities of death and separation. I sensed their frustration and anger over their feelings of helplessness and inadequacy. And I, too, felt helpless. I am glad now that I said nothing; that I was just there.

In practical terms, at times like these there are no adequate answers. We need to suspend judgment. We can say, "Lord, I'm so hurt, confused, even angry. I hate what's happening! There's no one to blame, so I feel like blaming You. I don't understand why You allowed this to happen. But I *do* understand why I trust You anyway. This doesn't mean You don't care or that something slipped through Your sovereign fingers. Life is ambiguous. It is simply what living in the gray zone is all about. Oh, God, would You comfort this family? Give us Your answers and bring us through this time."

When I pray in this way, I may not get an immediate answer from God, but something inside of me begins to relax. I experience His peace. By suspending judgment, I express my feelings, retain the integrity of my faith, and refuse to make a judgment.

That's what faith is all about.

But how do you handle the tough question of suffering in the world?

CHAPTER 5

THE PAINFUL QUESTION

"Pain insists upon being attended to.
God whispers to us in our pleasures,
speaks to us in our conscience,
but shouts in our pains:
It is His megaphone
to rouse a deaf world."
C. S. Lewis[1]

There has been a tragedy," Bill Bright told the 3,000 Campus Crusade for Christ staff members gathered in an auditorium in Colorado. "Some of our women are in the hospital, some are missing, and some have gone to be with the Lord." I was one of the missing.

The night before, on July 31, 1976, thirty-five Campus Crusade for Christ staff women were meeting at a ranch near the Big Thompson Canyon. Suddenly, with no prior warning, we heard a frantic voice yelling on a loud speaker, "Evacuate immediately! Get to higher ground! A flash flood is coming!"

What followed was a whirlwind of confusion, darkness, blinding rain, deafening thunder and shouting people. I escaped with seven other women by climbing a mountain in the down-pouring rain. Nineteen women in our group were trapped on the ranch. In the confusion, nine of the women in two cars headed the wrong direction. Their cars were swept into the raging waters as they were met broadside by the flood. Two of my friends were rescued; seven drowned. That night, 150 people lost their lives.

How tragic! What a seemingly senseless waste of human potential. Out of such experiences comes the almost intolerable question, "How can a good God allow suffering and evil in the world?" This *is* the painful question, and a cause of doubting for many people.

The problem of pain, in its simplest form, goes something like this: "If God were good, He would wish to make His creatures perfectly happy. And if God were almighty, He would be able to do what He wished. But the creatures are not happy. Therefore, God lacks either goodness or power, or both."[2]

Tough dilemma! This is the most daring question our faith will ever encounter. And it is instilled with power by the cries turned heavenward by every human being who ever lived. For no one passes through life unaffected by some measure of suffering.

In the midst of intense suffering, believers are tempted to curse God and give up their faith completely. Some do. Atheists, on the other hand, have been known to cry out in bitter anger toward this God they don't even believe exists. Never are Christians and atheists on more common ground.

Theologians and philosophers throughout the ages have grappled with this dilemma of suffering. Yet even the wisest sage falls immeasureably short of an emotionally and intellectually satisfying answer. Even addressing this subject often raises more questions than it answers.

I feel dwarfed by the magnitude of this question, and hardly adequate even to develop the problem, far less to provide satisfying answers. Therefore, I approach this matter as a fellow searcher. I know I can barely scratch the surface. My desire, however, is to offer a few simple insights that have helped me live with the painful reality of the presence of suffering and evil in the world.

The Painful Mystery

I love a good mystery. Give me a few Agatha Christie or Helen MacInnes novels, a warm blanket, a steaming pot of herbal tea, a blazing fire in the fireplace, and . . . so long! You won't see me for days. Mysteries intrigue me . . . as long as they are fiction.

In real life, however, I tolerate mystery poorly. That's why I struggled when I discovered that the problem of suffering and evil in the world is a mystery — a painful mystery. I can understand it to a point, but it will always contain an element of mystique. It always has; it always will.

Ironically, as I adjusted to this truth, I found in it a measure of comfort. I quit banging my head against the wall trying to find an absolute answer to a question that is inherently perplexing. I joined the ranks of the five billion other people who live with the quandary of the presence of suffering and evil in the world.

Webster defines *mystery* as "anything strange and inexplicable; a puzzle; a religious truth beyond human understanding."[3] Even the quantum theory in physics suggests that we can never understand the whole truth about everything. There is always an element of hidden information.

The Bible has much to say about mystery. Christ's indwelling of the believer is a mystery.[4] There is a mystery involved in understanding God's will.[5] Marriage, prayer, the unity of the body of Christ, the presence of evil in the world . . . each of these contains an element of mystery.

In the Bible, however, the word *mystery* suggests a progressive revealing of insights. Something is hidden but will be revealed by God at a future time. Or, in the present, the mystery will slowly be revealed to the believer as he seeks the Lord. The apostle Paul captures this idea when he says, "For now we see in a mirror dimly, but then face to face; now I know in part, but then I shall know fully" (1 Corinthians 13:12).

Mysteries, then, are those secrets about life that only God understands and that men desperately need to know but can't discover unless God reveals them.[6] For as Daniel says, "It is He who reveals the profound and hidden things" (Daniel 2:22).

I've grappled with this issue off and on for

seventeen years, sometimes with tears, and, at times, with a clenched fist. God has revealed some of the mystery, but the ultimate disclosure belongs in the category marked "To Be Revealed by God at a Future Time."

In the meantime, how have I lived with this painful reality? I began by admitting and learning to live with the truth that life is difficult. Jesus Himself said, "In the world you have tribulation" (John 16:33). Once I quit fighting this reality, I had energy to use more constructively. I began to cultivate the art of flexibility. I learned to live with ambiguity.

Also, when faced with the question, "How can a good God allow suffering and evil in the world?" I learned to suspend judgment.

Here's how it worked for me. Years ago, I chose a belief system that asserts God is good *and* God is omnipotent (almighty). Scripture strongly supports this belief; both aspects of His character are true.

I encountered problems, however, by putting these two attributes on a continuum. On one end I placed God's goodness; on the other, His omnipotence.

The misunderstanding came when I tried to balance the question of suffering and evil somewhere between these two attributes. If I let my finite reasoning slide too far toward the side of God's omnipotence, then I reasoned that God must be cruel or sadistic.

After all, if He is all-powerful, why doesn't He stop evil? God became like a policeman standing on a corner watching a crime take place. He had the power and authority to stop it, but He didn't.

If I let my reasoning slide too far toward the side of God's goodness, then I reasoned that God must be impotent. After all, if He is all good, but doesn't stop the evil, He must not have the power to do so. This is called "Santa Claus theology." God is good, loving and well-meaning, but impotent.

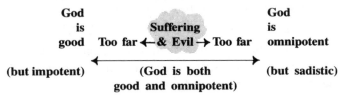

By seeing this issue on a continuum, I unknowingly forced myself to polarize my thinking. I also forced a separation between these two attributes of God, a separation that does not exist.

I have since come to see these two aspects of God's character, not on a continuum, but on two parallel lines going in the same direction. Somewhere between these two lines lies the mystery of suffering and evil.

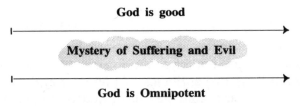

Before, I knew both God's goodness and His

omnipotence were absolutely and eternally true. Now I also understand that they do not oppose one another. Instead of the painful question *tearing apart* God's attributes, I now see it as being *contained* by all of them.

This perspective helped me to learn to suspend judgment. When reality threatens to force my logic toward the two extremes in the first diagram, I choose not to throw my personal belief system out the window. Instead, I refrain from drawing more conclusions than the evidence supports. As Os Guinness says, "Face to face with reality, and especially the mystery of evil, the faith that understands why it has come to trust must trust where it has not come to understand."[7]

People have asked me, "Were you afraid the night of the flood?" Yes, I was scared. Propane gas tanks that had been heating homes were smashing into rocks and exploding. The thunder was deafening. I was soaking wet and shivering uncontrollably as I helped an older woman climb the mountain. I was covered with mud when I found seven of my friends at the top of the mountain. At that time, we had lost contact with our other friends.

But that night, on top of that mountain, we chose to suspend judgment. That did not mean we denied reality. We hated what was happening. But we chose to trust God even though we didn't understand. One of my friends began praying, "Father, we don't understand this; we don't like it. But we trust You. You tell us that all things work together for good to those who love You.[8] And we do. Would

You work this together for good, even though it looks so bad?"

In essence, we said, "Lord, we do not understand what You are doing, but we know why we trust You in the first place. You love us. Therefore, we will trust You when we don't understand."

Life is difficult, and suffering is a mystery. But faith, knowing why it believes in the first place, can tolerate mystery.

The Price of Freedom

The Bible traces the entrance of suffering and evil into the world to a grand but potentially terrible quality of human beings: freedom. What makes man different from every other form of life is that he has true self-determining choice.

In President Reagan's second inaugural speech, on January 21, 1984, he said with great conviction, "Freedom is one of the deepest and noblest of all human desires."

To Americans, freedom is paramount. We sing about it, because it shows the dignity of man. We cry for it, because it shows the dignity of man. We die for it, because it shows the dignity of man. We wish freedom for all the people of the world because of our view of the dignity of man.

The President went on to say, "Freedom is the American song." He spoke about being "dedicated to the dreams of freedom *He* (God) has put into our heart."

Have you ever tried to explain the concept of

freedom to people who have never tasted it? I did one summer while vacationing in Poland. After a seven-mile hike, my friend Cynthia and I boarded a big raft, which would take us back to our beginning point. We were the only two Americans aboard; the rest were Polish. The only other person who spoke English was our interpreter.

It was beautiful and sunny as we floated down the river, which marked the border between Poland and Czechoslovakia. Our raft was full of laughter and singing. At one point, the people asked through our interpreter if we would sing some American songs. Since it was the Fourth of July, we chose to sing patriotic songs. Afterward, our interpreter asked us what the Fourth of July meant. I told her it was our Independence Day. I went on to explain how we had won freedom from England. Our form of government was now a democracy based on freedom of choice and responsibility.

As I saw her puzzled expression, I realized she had no experience to which she could relate this concept of freedom. She could not conceive of an alternate way of thinking or living. At that moment, my freedom became more precious to me.

But the gift of freedom carries a price tag. Free will is a two-edged sword. It implies choice; and choice implies alternatives. C. S. Lewis observed, "From the moment a creature becomes aware of God as God and of self as self, the terrible alternatives of choosing God or self for the center is open to it."[9]

Christian doctrine says that man chose to go his own independent way from God. This is known as the Fall (Genesis 3). This choice also is "the fall" in every individual life. A. W. Tozer says, "The moral shock suffered by us through our mighty break with God has left us all with a permanent trauma affecting every part of our nature. There is a disease, both in ourselves and in our environment."[10]

We have built a wall between us and God. Sometimes we choose God's way, sometimes we don't. He has given man the freedom to do what he wants, even to defy all the rules of the universe.

God, by His commitment to human freedom, imposed certain limits on Himself. Philip Yancey, in his book *Where is God When It Hurts?* suggests that whenever a creator enters a medium, he is limited by that medium.[11] He uses the example of wood. God created wood to be useful. He endowed it with certain properties: hardness, strength, flammability. These properties allow man to build homes for shelter, fires for warmth, and tools for work. But this same material, put into the hands of a person with free will, interjects danger. For that same piece of wood can now be used as a club to destroy another human being.

But can't God intervene? Yes, God *could* change the properties of wood into sponge every time man chose to use it destructively. But the logical conclusion of God intervening in every evil choice would be the eventual removal of choice altogether. Then we are back to where we started. No choice, no freedom.

So you see, freedom has a price. C. S. Lewis comments: "Christianity asserts that God is good . . . that one of the good things He made, namely the free will of rational creatures, by its very nature included the possibility of evil."[12]

The Presence of God

So far, we have approached, theologically and intellectually, the painful question of suffering. But that's far from where the question takes its toll. It strikes the greatest blow on the personal, emotional level. That's when, from the very core of our being, we cry out, "God, where are You? Where are You in my personal pain? It hurts so bad. Don't You care? God, why are You silent?"

Never is more demanded of our faith than when these questions engulf us. Never does it take more courage for faith to hold tight to *why* it has come to trust in the first place, and to suspend judgment.

Job, "the world's greatest sufferer," experienced success and failure in the face of unspeakable suffering. Most people do. With Job's first bout of disasters, the loss of his children and his fortune, the Bible pays him a high compliment: "Through all this Job did not sin nor did he blame God" (Job 1:22). At one point, after even greater suffering, Job's faith reached into his reservoir of courage as he cried out, "And as for me, I know that my Redeemer lives" (Job 19:25).

Yet in the midst of increased suffering, some scholars wonder if Job took his questioning too far and condemned God to justify himself.[13] His reaction, though wrong, is understandable. I often have done the same when it seemed the pressure would never end.

When this happens, where do I go for comfort? Where do I go to find answers to these haunting questions? I go to a person — Jesus Christ, and to an event in His life — the Crucifixion.

God is not silent. He entered history. He entered our stained, marred planet and He became a man. God didn't remain aloof from us. Rather, He had the integrity to enter human suffering and feel all that we feel. God Himself experienced love and loss, anger, rejection and pain. Even more incredible, He came to take upon Himself the combined effects of all the sin and evil in this world. When Jesus uttered on the cross, "It is finished," He was referring to the satisfaction of God's justice. Jesus satisfied it when He stood in our place and took upon Himself the full force of God's wrath against sin and evil.

The doctrine of God's wrath used to frighten me. Now that I understand it more, it actually brings me great comfort. You see, as Tozer puts it, "God's wrath is His utter intolerance of whatever degrades and destroys. He hates inequity as a mother hates the polio that would take the life of her child."[14]

God hates suffering and evil more than I do. But He did something about it — He sent His Son to die because of it. The death and resurrection of Jesus Christ broke the power of evil, undid the effects of the Fall, and opened the door for all time to anyone who will come to Him.

So God's wrath is His guarantee to me that evil has been defeated and that one day, after the last of those who are going to come to Him does come,

He will finally destroy all evil, wiping it from the face of the earth. Then He will usher in a whole new world, free from suffering and evil.

Although in my present circumstances, I may feel that God is silent, I know He hasn't always been silent. What He spoke then, He speaks today. What He spoke then stands for all eternity. He understands, He cares, and He did something about it. I am not alone.

But what about the question, Does God *will* suffering? I do not believe God arbitrarily sends suffering just to strengthen our faith or to drive sin from us, to humble us or to make us fit for extending love, compassion and comfort to others who are hurt. These things will result from trusting God through our suffering, but God does not *arbitrarily* will the suffering. Pain is simply a fact of life.

I correlate it to the human body's incredible pain system. When we hurt, our body is signaling us that something is wrong. Immediate attention is necessary.

When my friend Debbie doubled over in pain from intense abdominal cramping, we knew something was wrong. She was rushed to the hospital where the doctors diagnosed her as having a ruptured appendix. She was very sick, but she was treated in time and recovered.

In the same way, pain and suffering become God's megaphone to rouse a deaf world, to shatter the illusion that all is well in our world.[15] It usually causes us to turn to God for help. There is no substitute for His presence in our time of sorrow. We find solace in Jesus, "a man of sorrows, and acquainted with grief" (Isaiah 53:3).

We also can turn to our close friends for comfort. Oftentimes, when God seems far away, I experience His love and care through other believers. That's how God intended for the Body of Christ to function. Its members are to extend His love and grace to an evil world.

What breaks my heart, though, is to see the callousness often displayed verbally by well-meaning "comforters." They casually ask, "Have you prayed about it?" "Do you have any unconfessed sin in your life?" "Cheer up, things could be worse." "This is lasting so long; maybe you're not really trusting God." "I wonder what God is trying to teach you." People who counsel in this manner probably have never faced their own pain, so they do not know how to comfort others.

Do you know what I need most when I'm hurting? I need a warm hand; a friend to hold me when I cry; someone who will understand; and someone who will sit up with me all night if need be. You know the kind of friend I mean: someone to be angry with, someone to pray with, someone to help me not sink into passivity and bitterness, but rather to transform my suffering into strength, forgiveness and compassion.

The following excerpt from a recent article beautifully describes the meaning of Christ's suffering and offers hope for ours:

For the Christian, the theology of the cross and resurrection provides insight into the meaning of suffering . . . God did not send Jesus to the cross as a test of His faith, as punishment for His sin, or to build His character. The Romans crucified Jesus and made Him a victim of overt and deadly violence. It was a devastating experience for Jesus' followers who watched Him murdered . . . They left the scene of the crucifixion feeling abandoned and betrayed by God. The resurrection and the subsequent events were the surprising realization that in the midst of profound suffering, God is present and new life is possible. This retrospective realization in no way justified the suffering; it transformed it. It presented the possibility of new life coming forth from the pain of suffering. Sometimes Jesus' crucifixion is misinterpreted as being a model for suffering. Since Jesus went to the cross, according to the interpretation, a person should bear their own crosses of irrational violence . . . without complaint. Rather than the sanctification of suffering, Jesus' crucifixion remains a witness to the horror of violence. It is not a model of how suffering should be born, but a witness to God's desire that no one should have to suffer such violence again. The resurrection, the realization that . . . Christ was present to the disciples and is present to us, transformed the suffering and death experience. The people were set free from the pain of that experience to realize the newness of life among them.[16]

Where is God when we suffer? He is right alongside each one of us, hating evil and working to see its results transformed. God never sanctions evil; He transforms it. There is a painful mystery in life: the presence of suffering and evil. There is a price for the freedom God gives man: the possibility of evil. But there also is the presence of God, to transform our suffering.

I don't understand why God allowed that flood to take the lives of seven of my friends. I don't understand a lot about that night. It will forever remain a mystery to me. But I know one thing: That night I experienced the presence of the Lord in a way yet to be paralleled and never to be forgotten. That is enough for me.

"And as for me, I know that
my Redeemer lives" (Job 19:25).

CHAPTER 6

WHEN DARKNESS COMES

"In the world you have tribulation,
but take courage; I have overcome the world."
Jesus[1]

Courageous. That is how I would describe my friend Mary Graham. As the associate U. S. field director of Campus Crusade for Christ, her job involves long hours, a heavy workload and a high level of responsibility. Determination, a strong relationship with Christ, and courage keep her in the battle long after others would have quit, or at least requested a transfer.

But I have never seen Mary face anything with as much courage as she did the death of her parents. To lose one parent is incredibly difficult, but she lost both parents six weeks apart.

After seven years of recurring symptoms, Mary's mother was diagnosed as having Alzheimer's disease. What a hideous disease. Six months later, her father was diagnosed as having lung cancer. Both were given an indeterminate amount of time to live.

Then began the long, seemingly endless struggle. The following three years were a blur of doctors, hospitals, family consultations . . . and waiting. For Mary, it was excruciatingly painful to watch her parents deteriorate right before her eyes: her father physically, and her mother physically and mentally.

Mary's grief reached its zenith when her mother no longer recognized her. Mary had watched her become reduced from an active mother of seven to a "child" herself: helpless, dependent and unable to recognize her family. Mary was heartbroken.

That final year, Mary would work all week, then on Friday night drive the five hours to her parents' home to help care for them over the weekend. She did that numerous weekends, yet she rarely complained. Although she was exhausted, the Lord, courage, and love for her parents kept Mary going.

One day Mary received a call from her sister. Her mother had died in her sleep. Her father never got out of bed after that. Six weeks later, he died.

Mary was devastated. Darkness invaded her experience. She felt lifeless and depressed. Then, after experiencing the full force of her loss, loneliness and pain, grief's work was accomplished. Mary was ready to face the world again with a renewed sense of courage.

Loss of loved ones, floods, car accidents, rejection by friends, financial setbacks, marriage problems, child abuse and emotional problems are only a few of the many troubles people face in life. Christians are not exempt. The apostle Peter tells us, "Do not be surprised at the fiery ordeal among you, which comes upon you for your testing, as though some strange thing were happening to you" (1 Peter 4:12).

Difficulties and trials are part of the Christian life. Instead of becoming bitter or being destroyed by the doubts they can produce, Christians have the resources to come through these dark times with a greater depth of compassion, as well as with a stronger faith.

Since trials will come, how can we be ready for them? I believe we can prepare ourselves by recognizing that the Lord predicts trials, He gives permission for them, and He protects us in them.

Prediction Made

To say that the Lord predicts our trials may sound a little mystical. It means that, in His Word, He graciously gives us foreknowledge that trials will come.

For instance, James tells us to "consider it all joy . . . *when* [not if] you encounter various trials" (James 1:2). As we've seen, Peter tells us not to be surprised when trials come. And Jesus predicted that Peter would be tested and would deny Him three times.[2]

The Lord warns us about trials so that we can

prepare for them — mentally, emotionally, spiritually and physically — and therefore, not be caught off guard when they come.

The right perspective on trials is so important. Erwin Lutzer, in his book *Failure: the Backdoor to Success,* includes an excellent example:

> A coed wrote the following letter to her parents: "Dear Mom and Dad, Just thought I'd drop you a note to clue you in on my plans. I've just fallen in love with a guy called Jim. He quit high school after grade 11 to get married. About a year ago, he got a divorce. We've been going steady for two months and plan to get married in the fall. Until then, I've decided to move into his apartment (I think I might be pregnant). At any rate, I dropped out of school last week, although I'd love to finish college sometime in the future."

On the next page, the letter continued:

> "Mom and Dad, I just want you to know that everything I've written so far in this letter is false. NONE of it is true. But, Mom and Dad, it IS true that I got a "C" in French and flunked my math . . . it IS true that I'm going to need some more money for my tuition payments."[3]

After reading the letter's second page, her parents undoubtedly had a kindlier view of their daughter's academic shortcomings!

Perspective makes all the difference.

Two extremes in Christian thinking affect our perspective of the Christian life and lead to error. One extreme is the view that the Christian life is only exciting and abundant, and that if you're really walking with the Lord, that is all you will experience. The other extreme is that the Christian life is one big trial. Christians should be straight-laced, sober and sad, because they are in an endless war with sin and Satan.

J. I. Packer, in his book *Knowing God,* says, "It must be said that of these two extremes of error, the first is the worse, just to the extent that false hopes are a greater evil than false fears. The second error will, in the mercy of God, lead only to the pleasant surprise of finding that Christians have joy as well as sorrow. But the first, which pictures a normal Christian life as trouble-free, is bound to lead to bitter disillusionment sooner or later."[4]

Both extremes contain an element of truth. However, you must maintain those truths in balance. Then you will be prepared for trials and won't be as easily caught off guard. You will see your joys and difficulties in this moment of space we call time against the backdrop of an everlasting eternity. Both will be scaled down to a realistic perspective. Remember, the coed's *C* and *F* didn't look so bad when put in a different context. Neither will your trials.

Permission Granted

Nothing can happen to you unless God has granted permission. That means everything you go through and everything that comes your way comes directly from the hand of God. For instance, God gave permission for all of the trials Job experienced.[5] In another Scripture passage, we learn that the Lord gave permission for Satan to sift Peter like wheat.[6] Because God is sovereign, it stands to reason that nothing can touch us unless He allows it.

Hannah Smith sums up this truth beautifully:

> The question here confronts us at once. "But is God in everything and have we any warrant from the Scripture for receiving everything from His Hands without regarding the second causes that may have been instrumental in bringing them about?" I answer to this, unhesitatingly, "YES." To the children of God, everything comes directly from their Father's hand, no matter who or what may have been the apparent agents. There are no "second causes" for them. The whole teaching of Scripture asserts and implies this. "Second causes" must all be under the control of our Father, and not one of them can touch us except with His Knowledge and by His Permission."[7]

On the one hand, this truth brings a tremendous freedom and confidence. Nothing can happen to you by chance. Whatever comes your way, you can be sure it has been scrutinized and then allowed by your Heavenly Father.

But on the other hand, this truth raises a difficult question: You mean God, knowing the heartache, the pain, the nights of sleeplessness, and the hurt, gave permission for that to happen to me? Why?

This question has no pat answer, and it needs

to be dealt with very tenderly. To do so, I want to look at Peter's denial of Jesus in Luke 22:31-34. Ron Dunn, an excellent Bible teacher, explains that in this passage we see Jesus predicting Peter's failure, giving permission for it, and yet protecting Peter in it.

Jesus told Peter (predicted) that Satan had demanded permission to sift him like wheat. Instead of denying Satan permission, Jesus granted it. Why? The context gives two clues, which I believe can help Christians as they struggle with this issue in their own lives. These aren't the only reasons, but they are the two this passage gives.

We Learn from our Trials

The first reason is that Peter needed it. He didn't know his faith had some weak spots. Even after Jesus told Peter he would deny Him, the apostle's self-confidence wouldn't let him believe it. It seems that Peter's faith was more self-sufficient than God-dependent. The Lord knew that this kind of faith would never stand up against all that Peter would face in the years to come. But Peter didn't know that.

Genuine faith is faith that has been tested. And genuine faith is centered in the Lord, not in ourselves. In Hebrews 12:27, we are told that often God does what is needed to remove the things in our lives that can be shaken, in order that those things that cannot be shaken will remain.

You see, if I have subtly trusted in my good works, for example, or in the fact that I'm in full-time Christian work, the Lord, out of love, "shakes" me so I will move from this false security to trust in

Him alone. If my dependence has been on "good feelings," at times I may need to be deprived of those feelings to learn to depend on God only. When I have subtly felt that only my views about doctrine are correct, the Lord, in His mercy, has shaken me, at times plunging me into confusion to drive me back to Him alone.

Only God knows the faulty foundations upon which we depend. Only He knows that in the end, if we continue to trust in these props, we will not withstand the pressures of life.

I have discovered that I don't usually trust God until I have to. As Ron Dunn says, "Jesus is all you need, but until He's all you've got . . . you don't know it."

So, like Peter, at times we fail. Peter did deny Christ, and when all hope was gone "he went outside and wept bitterly" (Luke 22:62). Some things we learn only through failure. But when all hope is gone, we still have God . . . and we find He is enough.

Others Benefit from our Trials

Not only did Peter need his faith to be tested, but the second reason for God's testing was that others needed it, too. Jesus knew that Peter would fail. He also knew that once the apostle turned back to Him, he would strengthen the other Christians.[8] Times of intense persecution were ahead for the church; men and women with a God-centered faith were needed.

The apostle Paul tells us that God "comforts us

in all our afflictions so that we may be able to comfort those who are in any affliction with the comfort with which we ourselves are comforted by God" (2 Corinthians 1:4).

Have you ever prayed, "Lord, do whatever You need to do in my life to make me usable for Your Kingdom"? I have. Do you know how He does that? Often, He makes us usable by taking us through difficult times, which tenderize our hearts and equip us with empathy and compassion for others. He takes us through those times, not arbitrarily, but with our highest good in mind.

I often discover, though, that when He starts to answer my prayer, I forget my altruistic motives and begin yelling, "Stop! I've had enough. I don't care about other people." However, God knows what we need, and He knows what others need. So He works both these needs together beautifully, neither at the expense of the other.

This means we also can benefit from the results of others' trials. When I hurt very deeply, as I have a number of times, I go to someone who I know cares about me and who knows what it's like to hurt — someone who is not judgmental, but tender.

One summer, I felt that my world was shattered. Unexpected, tragic news had broken my heart. To make matters worse, my roommate was out of town for months, so I was living alone.

I will never forget the love and care extended to me by Ney Bailey and Mary Graham. They bundled me up and took me home with them, and I stayed for two weeks. They cried with me, prayed with me, and listened as I tried to express my hurt. In essence, they comforted me. I know that was possible only because of what they had come through in their own lives. From that special experience, I learned never to take lightly the price someone else has paid to comfort me.

At times we go through tragedies in life and never really know why. It may be that, as Ron Dunn says, in eternity we will see, in the life of someone, why.

These two reasons for God's testing — our need and the need of others — are not catchalls in which to stuff all the world's suffering. Sometimes we just don't know why things happen. I am learning that the bottom line of faith is not to answer all of my doubts, but to make me sure of God. So, in the face of unanswered "whys," once again I suspend judgment.

Protection Insured

I could not have been more than three or four years old when my fear of crickets reached its peak. As darkness fell and they began their familiar singing, my fear rose. One summer evening, I was all ready for bed in my favorite yellow pajamas (the ones with the little feet), when my dad picked me up and took me outside. Very protectively, he sat me on his knee and put his arms around me. Then he began telling me all about crickets and how they make "that noise." The longer I sat enfolded in my father's arms, listening to him talk, the less afraid I became. After all, in my father's arms, there wasn't a cricket in the world that could hurt me. My protection was insured.

When darkness comes into our lives, our protection is insured. The Scriptures tell us that God is our deliverer and our shield.[9] The Lord promises never to leave us or forsake us.[10] Jesus Himself prays for us.[11] Just think of it: God, the Creator, the Almighty God, has committed Himself to our protection.

When Jesus predicted that Peter would deny Him, He added, "But I have prayed for you" (Luke 22:32). Putting the whole passage together, it looks like this: Jesus knew what was going to happen (He predicted it); the whole situation was in His Hands (He gave permission for it); and He prayed for Peter (He provided protection) — before it ever happened.

If we can begin to take in the significance of this! Jesus knew that Peter would fail Him, though Peter didn't. God was not surprised. And sure enough, Peter denied the Lord not once but *three* times. Immediately following Peter's third denial, Jesus, under arrest, "turned and looked at Peter" (Luke 22:61). At that moment, Peter remembered the Lord's prediction and was cut to the core. He wept bitterly.

But even in his failure, Peter was not alone. Not only did Jesus pray for him, but when He looked at Peter, I believe He was also reaching out to him with eye contact. Jesus didn't have to look at Peter, but He did. And I don't believe it was an "I told you so" look. I have a hunch Jesus wanted Peter to remember not just part of His prediction but all of it.

It's as though the Lord said with one glance,

"Remember that I have prayed for you, Peter, and *when* [not *if*] you return, you will strengthen your brethren. It's OK, Peter. I'm going ahead to forgive you. Soon you will know."

Peter was a loved man. But at that moment of denying Christ, all he experienced was utter disillusionment, guilt and, I'm sure, hopelessness.

But after death, there is resurrection. And when Christ arose, the disciples exclaimed, "The Lord has really risen, and has appeared to Simon (Peter)" (Luke 24:34). I can barely imagine the joy that must have exploded in Peter's heart.

Whatever darkness we go through, and whatever doubts come our way because of the trials, we can be sure Jesus is praying for us. In addition, Jesus never sends us anywhere that He doesn't go with us. Our protection is insured.

Within three guesses, I can predict somewhat accurately where you are right now. Either you are just coming out of a difficult time; or you are in the midst of a difficult time; or, finally, you will be in a difficult time in the near future.

The following suggestions may be helpful when your personal darkness comes.

1. Settle in your mind that there are no "second causes" in the Christian life. Everything comes from the hand of your loving, heavenly Father.

2. Tell the Lord exactly how you feel. Don't be afraid to express all your questions and feelings.

3. The most difficult thing to do is to thank

the Lord. God's Word says, "In everything give thanks; for this is God's will for you in Christ Jesus" (1 Thessalonians 5:18). Notice this doesn't say we are to thank the Lord *for* everything (remember, evil forever remains evil), but we are to thank Him *in the midst* of everything. At times, we may not feel thankful, but to give thanks anyway expresses our confidence that God is in control. It also helps to protect us from bitterness.

4. Continue getting to know the Lord better and better. You can only trust someone as far as you know him.

5. Surround yourself with people who love you. You will need their care and support.

The Christian life involves joy and sorrow. To embrace them both and learn the lessons contained in each is rare. It takes courage. But it brings tremendous rewards.

I am grateful for my time of darkness. Doubt was a good teacher, for out of it came one of the most valuable lessons I have learned in life: People grow better in grace.

CHAPTER 7

PEOPLE GROW BETTER IN GRACE

*"So few people have any conception of what
the grace of God really is."
Hannah Whitall Smith[1]*

Imagine standing in a registration line at your local college or university campus. Wanting to improve your communication skills, you have decided to enroll in Speech 101. You see in the registration booklet that this class is taught by two professors: Dr. Grace and Dr. Law.

Being unfamiliar with either professor, you tap the shoulder of the guy in front of you. "Excuse me, have you had classes taught by either Dr. Grace or Dr. Law?"

"Sure," the fellow answers. "I've had classes

from both those professors."

"What are they like?"

"Dr. Law is really a case. His content is good, but that's about it. He's hard-nosed. I found him to be rigid, demanding and impossible to please. What really irked me was that he constantly pointed out every little place you failed or fell short. What a trip!

"But Dr. Grace . . . well, I really like the guy. Not only is his content good, but he's very encouraging. Now he's no pushover; he really knows his stuff. Yet he's supportive and helpful. What really impressed me was how he seemed to do everything he could to help make a student successful. Yeah, he's a good prof."

From which instructor would you take Speech 101? I would choose Dr. Grace. In fact, I would do anything to get into his class.

Yet, often in our Christian growth, and in the development of our faith, we choose just the opposite. We try to grow by subjecting ourselves to the rigid, demanding standard of the Law. We subtly think, "I need to do all these things to grow and I need to stop doing all these other things." This rigid environment is a breeding ground for doubt, for, despite our sincere and diligent efforts, we never satisfy the Law.

God has given only one avenue to growth: grace. The apostle Peter tells us we are to "grow in the grace and knowledge of our Lord and Savior Jesus Christ" (2 Peter 3:18). To grow, we must choose God's way — through grace — because people grow better in grace.

Grace Is Fertile Soil

People grow better in grace, because grace is fertile soil. It is fertile by its very nature.

Defined theologically, grace is the "spontaneous, self-determined kindness of God," or the "free, un-merited favor of God." In other words, grace simply means giving us what we don't deserve.

But a theological definition can leave me cold. Hannah Smith puts "arms" on grace when she says, "To say that it (grace) is free, unmerited favor only expresses a little of its meaning. It is the unhindered, wondrous, boundless love of God poured out upon us in an infinite variety of ways without stint or measure not according to our deserving but according to His measureless heart of love which passes knowl-edge . . . so unfathomable are its heights and depths."[2]

Now that's fertile soil! Planted in that environ-ment, who wouldn't grow? If we had even one friend with a small measure of that kind of love and accep-tance, there would be no limit to our growth. God designed grace to be the basis for healthy growth. If we miss grace, we've missed it all.

Grace is also fertile soil because it focuses on who God is and what He has done, and it takes the focus off ourselves. In fact, when we see who God is, we discover our own spiritual bankruptcy. And that is grace: seeing our need for Him.

I remember my close friend Carolyn gently say-ing to me, "Life is learning that we are God-dependent and not self-sufficient. All we need for living the Christian life comes from Him, not from ourselves. Jackie, I think you try too hard." I knew she was right.

It's so easy to think we must *do* something to earn God's favor. It's as though grace is too good to be true.

That's exactly where the Galatian Christians found themselves in the first century. Having begun their relationship with Christ firmly planted in grace, they were now being influenced by outsiders to think that salvation and Christian growth depended upon certain forms and ceremonies (keeping the Law).

Paul confronts this heresy head-on with his powerful thesis statement in Galatians 5:1: "It was for freedom that Christ set us free; therefore keep standing firm and do not be subject again to a yoke of slavery."

Paul says that trying to keep the Law as a means of salvation or growth is a yoke of slavery. He goes on to explain that when a person trusts in a ceremonial practice (the Law) to gain acceptance with God, then he is under obligation to keep all of the laws of the Old Testament. But no one can keep *all* of God's laws. And when a person tries, he will find himself cut off from the grace of Christ.[3] For God's grace is for those who depend upon God for salvation, rather than on their own efforts and deeds.

Freedom, according to Paul, is dependence upon the Spirit of God for our right standing with God, as well as for our growth.[4] What a contrast! Freedom through being God-dependent and not self-sufficient takes us instantly off of a performance basis with

God. The focus in the Christian life then shifts from keeping a list of do's and don'ts to relating to a person — Jesus Christ. That's freedom, and Paul exhorts the Galatians to stay firmly planted in the soil of freedom and grace.

Yet, everything in society fights against this freedom. Sadly, even in our Christian lives, we add rules and expectations to ourselves and others, which leads us to perform for acceptance.

Early in my working career, I had a boss who epitomized the Law. He held to numerous spoken and unspoken rules.

One such rule was that I needed to have my lights out by 11 P.M. so I would not be tired on the job the next day. Unfortunately, my house was not far from his, and if he happened to notice my light on after 11, I heard about it the next morning in meetings.

Up until the end of that year, I don't remember one compliment from my boss. However, he was liberal with complaints and criticisms of my work.

Then came my first compliment from him.

I had been given a project over which I had complete ownership. I worked night and day to make it better than perfect and thus win his approval.

On the day of the event, he wanted all of the other employees to arrive an hour early to help with the preparations. Even after I explained that coming early would not be necessary, he insisted. After the employees stood around for an hour with nothing to do, the program began. I couldn't have been more pleased with the event. The project was flawless.

Afterward, my boss walked up to me, looked down at the floor, and out of his mouth came the long-awaited words, "Well done, Miss Hudson."

How did I respond to my year in this environment? I could sum it up in one word: vengeance. You see, the Law, which my boss epitomized, only incites rebellion, and I rebelled.

But grace engenders love and freedom. Grace is fertile soil, and people grow better in grace.

The Law Grows the Fruit of Legalism

One day I asked a few of my friends in full-time Christian work for their first and uncensored response to the question: "How would you feel today if you didn't read your Bible?" Three people answered with one word: "guilty." One said, "I would feel like something is missing."

Then I asked myself the same question, and my honest response was, "guilty." I wondered why. I knew my sins had been forgiven. I knew how to walk in the power of the Holy Spirit. I knew I was accepted completely. But somehow I still subtly thought that surely God would be more pleased if I read my Bible every day. Why was that?

I believe the answer is the subtle creeping in of a legal spirit, better known as legalism. Legalism is an outlook on life in which a person seeks to find acceptance with God (justification) or to grow (sanctification) by his works (his own efforts in keeping the Law). But the Law only grows the fruit of legalism.

It is not that the Law is bad. The Law is good, but how we regard the Law makes all the difference. Paul explains that the Law is like our tutor. It shows how far we fall short of God's righteous standard. Then it graciously points us to Christ, "that we may be justified by faith" (Galatians 3:24). The Law is like a thermometer; it doesn't make us well; it only tells us we are sick.

In the life of a Christian, when the Law becomes the focus, it only produces legalism. A speaker once said, "The Law moves us from the rock of God's grace into the swamp of self-effort."

Paul made an eye-opening observation about self-effort and the Christian life. He wrote: "A little leaven leavens the whole lump of dough" (Galatians 5:9). This means that just as a little yeast can affect the whole loaf of bread, so a little self-effort will grow and eventually permeate a person's entire Christian life. Before long, he will find himself laboring under the weight of trying to keep the entire Old Testament Law. The burden is overwhelming. And since he never can fulfill the Law, he will doubt God's love and acceptance.

Legalism, in essence, is trying to add something to the finished work of Christ. The Jews of the first century added ceremonies; Christians throughout the centuries have added some ridiculous rules. Today we add resolutions, Christian service, church attendance, good feelings, right doctrine. These are important, but only as the result of growth, not as a means to it.

Hannah Smith says, "It does not make much difference what you add; it is wrong to add anything at all. Legal Christians do not deny Christ; they only seek to add something to Christ. Their idea is Christ and — something besides. Perhaps it is Christ and good works, or Christ and earnest feelings."[5]

Paul's response to people adding anything to the work of Christ was not exactly mild.

> But even though we, or an angel from heaven, should preach to you a gospel contrary to that which we have preached to you, let him be accursed (Galatians 1:8).
> You foolish Galatians, who has bewitched you . . .? This is the only thing I want to find out from you: did you receive the Spirit by the works of the Law, or by hearing with faith? (Galatians 3:1,2)
> Would that those who are troubling you would even mutilate themselves (Galatians 5:12).

It is imperative to recognize when you are slipping off the rock of God's grace into the swamp of self-effort. The clues are different for everyone, but I have found four patterns that emerge in my life as warnings that I'm headed for the swamp.

Pitfalls of Legalism

I call the first pattern the "should cycle." It goes something like this: "I should be better. I should have done better. I should be able to do better in the future." I feel that I've never done quite enough. When I begin to fall into the should cycle, I'm beginning to look to myself for approval instead of to God.

My second pattern is that of self-deprecation. Very subtly I begin to turn on myself, saying, "I can't believe you did that! You are so stupid. Won't you ever learn?" The negative, downward spiral begins, and before long I feel like a complete failure. When I see this pattern developing, I realize I've taken my eyes off God's grace and have begun focusing on my self-effort.

The age-old "performance syndrome" is the third pattern I fall into. I begin performing again to gain approval. I do more, hoping to feel better. But when I do this, I inevitably set myself up for failure because I can never do enough. Before long, I'm tired and I rebel at my own expectations. For instance, if I demand of myself, "Today I will go on a diet," by dinner I manage to blow it. When I feel this pressure to perform, I know I'm slipping off the rock of grace.

When all else fails, I hide. This is the final pattern that warns me I'm sinking fast into the swamp of self-effort, and I don't want to admit it. When I blow it, grace gives me freedom to confess my sin and grow. The law condemns me, making me want to hide.

When my younger sister and I were four and seven years old, we decided to play "Tarzan" on our twin beds while our parents were out. First, she would pound her chest, giving a great Tarzan yell, and jump from her headboard onto her mattress. Then it was my turn, and I followed suit. Finally, we had a brainstorm and decided to both jump from her headboard onto her mattress. We flew through the air, and our now-perfected Tarzan yells completely drowned out the sound of breaking boards as wooden slats, mattress, Sandy and I all fell to the floor. The babysitter never heard a thing.

Afraid of the law, "Don't jump on the beds!" we immediately began to hide the evidence. I had Sandy get in bed with me, I turned out the lights, and we pretended to be asleep. When we heard our parents come home, Sandy got out of bed and jumped on her bed again to make a loud noise. Quickly, she got under her covers to pretend she had been sleeping when "all of a sudden" the bed broke.

Mom and Dad flew into our room, switched on the light, and saw both of us "sound asleep" in our beds. How they ever saw through my ingenious plan, I'll never know. But our attempt to hide and cover our error was foiled.

When I find myself hiding, putting on a mask, not wanting to admit my failure, not wanting to own up to my inadequacies, wanting to appear perfect, I know I'm swimming hard in the swamp of self-effort.

Ray Stedman calls this the "Great Masquerade." "In order to be liked or accepted we must appear capable or successful. [But God's way] is if we will admit our inadequacy, we can have God's adequacy, and all we have sought vainly to produce is given to us at the point of our inability."[6]

When I find myself flirting with legalism, I usually stop and confess to the Lord my self-sufficient attitude. I remind myself that I'm God-dependent and not self-sufficient. I remember that all I need for living the Christian life comes from God and not from myself.

Then I remind myself of the difference between law and grace. Hannah Smith, in her book *The Christian's Secret of a Happy Life,* describes it this way:[7]

LAW	*GRACE*
1. The LAW says: "DO *this* and you will live."	1. GRACE says *"LIVE* and then you will do."
2. The LAW says: *"PAY* me what you owe me."	2. GRACE says: "I freely *FORGIVE* you all."
3. The LAW says: *"MAKE* yourself a new heart and a new spirit."	3. GRACE says: "A new heart will I *GIVE* you and a new spirit will I put within you."
4. The LAW says: *"YOU SHALL LOVE* the Lord your God with all your heart and with all your soul and with all your mind."	4. GRACE says: "Here is love, not that we loved God but that *HE LOVED* us and sent His Son to be the propitiation (payment substitute) for our sins."
5. The LAW says: "The *WAGES* of sin is death."	5. GRACE says: "The *GIFT* of God is eternal life through Jesus Christ our Lord."

6. The LAW *DEMANDS* holiness.	6 .GRACE *GIVES* holiness.
7. The LAW says: *"DO."*	7 .GRACE says: *"DONE."*
8. The LAW makes blessings the result of *OBEDIENCE.*	8 .GRACE makes obedience the result of *BLESSINGS.*
9. The LAW says: *"IF . . ."*	9 .GRACE says: *"THEREFORE . . ."*
10. The LAW was given for the *RESTRAINT* of the old man.	10. GRACE was given to bring *LIBERTY* to the new man.
11. Under the LAW, salvation was *WAGES.*	11. Under GRACE, salvation is a *GIFT.*

No wonder Paul wants us to stay planted in the soil of God's grace!

Grace Grows the Fruit of Freedom

Paul claims that Christians are "Called to freedom" (Galatians 5:13). Freedom from the law, freedom from the bondage of sin, and freedom from self-effort are all results of being planted in the soil of God's grace.

Elisabeth Elliot, in her book *The Liberty of Obedience,* included this comment:

"I am in earnest about forsaking 'the world' and following Christ. But I am puzzled about worldly things. What is it I must forsake?" a young man asks.

"Colored clothes, for one thing. Get rid of everything in your wardrobe that is not white. Stop sleeping on a soft pillow. Sell your musical instruments and don't eat any more white bread. You cannot, if you are sincere about obeying Christ, take warm baths or shave your beard. To shave is to lie against Him who created us, to attempt to improve on His work."

Does this answer sound absurd? It is the answer given in the most celebrated Christian schools of the second century! Is it possible that the rules that have been adopted by many twentieth century Christians will sound as absurd to earnest followers of Christ a few years hence?[8]

These particular second century Christians missed the freedom available through God's grace. How sad that today many Christians are still missing this freedom. Perhaps it is because mankind has an incurable bent toward legalism. All I know is it has taken me years to begin realizing that God is gentle, not harsh; He is my Father, not my taskmaster. God forgives my sin; He does not hold it against me. He wants a relationship with me, not only my service. That is freedom.

Paul tells us that the key to freedom is walking in the Spirit.[9] And we walk in the Spirit by faith. In Ephesians 5:18, Paul commands believers to be filled with the Spirit. And 1 John 5:14,15 gives us God's promise that if we ask anything according to His will, He hears us and will answer our prayer. Faith, then, takes God at His Word and asks to be filled with the Spirit. Faith rests, believing God has done what He promised.

Walking in the Spirit also is realizing, moment by moment, that we are totally dependent on another's power for living the Christian life. This dependency on God is not to be confused with an infant's helpless dependency on his parents before he has the ability of choice. Rather, it is a responsible choice we make to depend upon God as the source of our spiritual life.

Finally, walking in the Spirit involves relaxing in the process. Miles Stanford, in his powerful book *The Green Letters,* says, "It seems that most believers have difficulty in realizing and facing up to the inexorable fact that God does not hurry in His development of our Christian life. He is working from and for eternity!"[10] People don't stumble into maturity. Growth takes time.

The greatest principle God uses in our growth is need. I hate to feel needy. It makes me feel out of control. Yet I'm learning not to run from my need, but rather to let it draw me to Christ, who has promised to meet all my needs.[11] When I come to Him, I see my own spiritual bankruptcy, but I also begin to discover the riches He has available for me. Sometimes I wonder if the reason I don't experience more of God's power at times is because I am not aware enough of my spiritual need and helplessness. Paul says, "For when I am weak, then I am strong" (2 Corinthians 12:10).

I continually am learning the lesson that I'm God-dependent and not self-sufficient, and that I will have to walk in the Spirit the rest of my life. A healthy child eventually outgrows dependence upon his parents, but as children of God, we grow daily in our awareness of our dependence upon God as the source of spiritual life. We will never mature to the point that we don't need God.

I fly a lot in my job and, as a result, I practically have the flight attendant's speech memorized. I know where all the exits are; I know how to use the oxygen masks; I know every normal noise and movement of the plane. But even with my vast knowledge, I could never imagine the following scene.

We have just reached our cruising altitude of 35,000 feet when I motion to the flight attendant. "I think I'm ready," I tell her. "You see, I have flown hundreds and thousands of miles, and I'm ready to fly. If you don't mind opening the door, I'll try my wings."

With a shrug of her shoulders and a "to each his own" under her breath, the flight attendant opens the door and I step out. For 34,999 feet I would remain airborne. Then, in one quick instant, I would lose my credibility. You see, no matter how long I've flown, I am still unable to fly without the plane.

It is the same in the Christian life. When I became a Christian seventeen years ago, I was placed into Christ. No matter how long I've walked with Him, there will never come a time when I will "fly" on my own. I believe God wants us to soar, to be overcomers, to be victorious, but not in ourselves — in Him.

Have you been *trying* to grow in your Christian life? Acknowledge your spiritual bankruptcy. Acknowledge your dependency on Christ, and by faith, ask Him to fill you with His Spirit. Then fly!

Once, after I spoke on the subject of grace, someone from the audience came up to me and asked, "If you only talk about grace, aren't you afraid people will sin more? Don't you think it will lead to license?"

This question reflects the common error of putting legalism on one end of a continuum and license on the other, and then trying to balance grace somewhere between the two. A person may indeed struggle by going back and forth between legalism and license. And that is definitely a problem concerning self-effort or sin that needs to be dealt with. But grace doesn't even belong on the continuum!

Understanding grace takes us off the continuum of self-effort and sin and places us into Christ, where we find the power, energy and love with which to face life. It also causes us to be deeply grieved by our sin and the sin we see around us. Understanding grace and freedom does not decrease responsibility — it increases it. With freedom comes responsibility.

The people I've seen who have been touched by God's grace have a deep sense of freedom and joy. They also have a corresponding sense of responsibility to the Lord and to the world around them. The key is that they know how to handle this responsibility through faith in Him.

Grace is fertile soil where freedom can blossom and grow.

Growing Through Grace

I wish you knew my sister Sandy. She is quite a woman. Difficult experiences mark her past. During a confused, painful time in her life, she resorted to immorality, drugs and alcohol. When these things no longer dulled the pain, she tried to take her life. She failed. Eventually, as the pain mounted, she again attempted suicide. Fortunately, she failed once again and was rushed to a hospital. Broken, confused and lost, she returned home.

Having become Christians and having learned from past mistakes, family members now surrounded her with love and grace. No one said, "I told you so," or "It's about time you came to your senses." Rather, she was met with God's grace through people who loved her.

Six months later, Sandy committed her life to Christ and experienced His grace personally. Her spiritual, physical and emotional recovery was slow, but definite.

Do you know what Sandy's favorite song is? "Amazing Grace": "Amazing grace, how sweet the sound . . . ! I once was lost but now I'm found, was blind, but now I see." Today, Sandy is secure in her walk with the Lord. She is enrolled in a Bible class and helps other women grow in their faith. She has a wonderful Christian husband and two fantastic children. Sandy has taught me much about life and grace. I see a depth in her that I rarely see in others.

Life is not a bed of roses for Sandy and her family by any means. They have problems like anyone else. But they know how to stay planted in the soil of His grace.

If you were to meet my sister and sit down across the table from her to share a pot of coffee, do you know what she would do? She would look you straight in the eyes and say, "People grow better in grace!"

CHAPTER 8

LET'S GET PRACTICAL

*"We must resort to habit once the mind has seen where
the truth lies, in order to steep and stain ourselves
in that belief which constantly eludes us."*

Pascal[1]

How do you respond to the advice, 'Confess doubt as sin, and decide once and for all you will never doubt again'?"

I was near the end of my interview with Dr. Cyril Barber, a scholar and author, when I asked this question. Looking me straight in the eyes, he teasingly replied, "Do you actually want me to put my comments on tape?"

I smiled and nodded. "Yes."

Barely pausing, he continued, "Such things (and you're right, they have appeared in books) are theologically stupid . . . stupid . . . stupid! . . . because no one can resolve never to doubt again."

I felt like cheering. Instead, I retained my neutral interviewer's demeanor and encouraged him to continue. (He needed no encouragement.)

"It's not in us. Our frailty and the effects of sin in our lives have so devastated us that we will be hedged about by doubts and fears all our lives. So, theologically, that advice is very inappropriate.

"Psychologically, it is devastating. You create in people expectations which are going to be shattered in the future and that will only increase their feelings of guilt and misgiving and destroy any sense of worth that had been built up. It is a tragedy that this advice ever appeared in print and I wish it had never seen the light of day. Those who conceived of it had a utopian expectation of perfection that they themselves could never live up to. Now, that's on tape!"[2]

Doubts do not go away simply because a person decides never to doubt again. He must instead face them squarely and find healthy, constructive and practical avenues toward resolution.

Where Doubt Originates

Generally speaking, doubt stems from our humanness. Even so, its origin in a life can be traced back to a number of issues. I have divided these issues into seven areas. They are not hard and fast, nor necessarily exhaustive, but they do consistently emerge. Doubt can stem from:

1. a faulty foundation

2. an inaccurate view of God

3. immorality

4. faith being tested

5. spiritual warfare

6. damaged emotions

7. the normal growth process

In resolving doubt, it helps to identify the specific root of your doubt. Then you can begin to apply a specific solution.

In this chapter, I will offer explanations and suggestions for the first three areas that give rise to doubt. These deal with issues somewhat within the doubters' power to control. In the next chapter, I'll cover the last four areas, which to a degree, reach beyond the doubters' control. The person has been or is being acted upon by influences outside himself, and doubt results.

A Faulty Foundation

Few people would build a house without laying the proper foundation. Jesus said a man who builds a house upon the sand is foolish, because when the first real storm hits, the house crumbles.[3]

The first category of doubt sources deals with this very issue: a faulty foundation. This is a breeding ground for doubt, especially when one faces the mysteries of life.

I believe two elements constitute a faulty foundation. The first is not knowing *what* or *why* you believe. People place their faith in Christ for any number of reasons, and many trust Christ as their personal Savior without really knowing the full implications of *what* they believe. Nor do they understand *why* it is reasonable to believe. For a faith that will ultimately stand up against the pressures of living, however, we need to build a foundation of knowing what we believe and why. Not to do so is to build our faith on sand.

Do You Know What You Believe?

Richard is a successful businessman in his mid-forties. I listened intently as he expressed his doubts about the validity of Christianity. Three years earlier, he had committed his life to Christ during a particularly difficult crisis in his life. There is no question that his commitment was sincere. And in a very real and personal way, the Lord met him in his deep need and walked through it with him.

But now, Richard found himself doubting, and this greatly disturbed him. I knew he was getting reputable help for a number of personal tragedies in his past, so that base was covered. I also knew he attended church every Sunday, so he was getting some spiritual input. Beyond that, in the past three years he had had very little teaching regarding his faith. He was trying to build his entire Christian life on his initial emotional experience of being met by the Lord. Although valid, he needed to know more about who God was, exactly what he believed, and the verifiable reasons for his beliefs.

Wisely, Richard placed himself in a discipleship setting to learn more about the person and work of Jesus Christ, the basic doctrines that make Christianity unique yet universal, and the historical evidence surrounding the Christian faith. I believe Richard faces a one- to three-year process of making the foundation of his faith strong so it will sustain him the rest of his life.

A person who lacks sufficient reason for believing will not have sufficient reason to keep believing when difficulties arise. When he doesn't understand what God is doing, or when he is confronted with an agnostic's cynical questions, his faith will falter. This is where doubt enters.

But Christianity is reasonable, for it is based on truth. It is not true simply because I choose to believe it's true. The truth of Christianity is an objective reality whether I choose to believe it or not. Likewise, as Os Guinness writes, "Christianity is not true because it works; it works because it is true."[4]

Contrary to many skeptics' claims, God never demands anyone to commit intellectual suicide to believe. Faith and reason are not diametrically opposed. Rather, they are an extension of each other. They are allies. Faith can operate because we have reason to believe; and because we have reason to believe, faith can operate where our reason leaves off. Unless we have evidence to believe God on a basic level, we will not trust Him for what we cannot understand and for what goes beyond our finiteness. As a popular poster states, "Because of what I have seen, I can trust my Creator for what I have not seen."

Faith and reason go hand in hand, supporting and giving credence to one another. When reason reaches its limit and can take us no further, our faith can take over and sustain us. You see, as Os Guinness says, "Faith does not feed on thin air but on facts. Its instinct is to root itself in reality, and it is this which distinguishes faith from fantasy."[5]

Thus to deal with this kind of doubt, you need to know what and why you believe. Reading and studying will help greatly. A good place to start is with the Christian classics, biographies of great men and women of faith, and the superb collection of Christian apologetics available today. (A suggested reading list is included at the end of the book.)

It also might be helpful to enroll in a class or, like Richard, join a discipleship group aimed at studying the basics of the Christian faith. Building a strong foundation will be worth every bit of effort. A person without good reason to believe has good reason to doubt.

Are You Committed to What You Believe?

A second element of a faulty spiritual foundation is a lack of commitment. A Christian without commitment and conviction can have only a mediocre, apathetic faith. His feet are firmly planted nowhere.

I have a fear of mediocrity. The last thing I want is to get to the end of my life and realize I haven't given it my best shot. I doubt anyone *plans* to live a mediocre life. It just happens, unless we plan otherwise.

Mediocrity can surface as boredom with one's faith or doubt about the validity of what he believes. "How do I know all of this is true?" he may ask. "My life seems no different from anyone else's." These questions are not altogether bad, for if they trouble him enough, they may drive him to examine the level of his conviction.

As explained earlier, this type of doubt has nothing to do with the validity of what is believed. It has everything to do with the believer taking responsibility for his choice to believe. His discontent is not *outside* himself, in what he believes, but rather *within,* in his lack of commitment to it.

Doubt related to lack of commitment may or may not be intentional. A person may adopt his parents' faith without examining it. Or perhaps he fears what God might ask him to do. More critically, a person may consciously choose to live with a mediocre faith. He may think, *I'll get serious about God when I'm older, or when my children are older, or when my business is off the ground and running.*

Solving this type of doubt requires an act of your will. As Fenelon, one of the fathers of our faith, claims, "Pure religion resides in the will alone."[6] The doubter must choose to get off the fence and commit himself fully to God.

Paul calls for this kind of decision in Romans 12:1: "I urge you . . . by the mercies of God, to present your bodies a living and holy sacrifice, acceptable to God." First, you should examine your faith.

Then, as you come to realize that what you believe is fact and not fantasy, and you recognize it is indeed safe to commit yourself to a God who loves you so totally, you can, as an act of your will, get off the fence and yield yourself completely to God.

This is what Paul is urging in Romans 12:1. In response, you can surrender by a simple act of faith through prayer. You might say, "Lord, I recognize that my doubt has come from a lack of commitment. Forgive me. Now, by faith, I give myself completely to You. I don't want to sit on the fence any longer. I want You to be Lord of my life. Thank You for answering my prayer."

No one would purposely sit in a chair that has three or four weak legs. It would not hold them. In the same way, if our faith is built upon a faulty foundation, it will not hold us in the long run. That is why we must rebuild it. It is never too late to go back and start over, making the foundation of our faith strong.

An Inaccurate View of God

How would you describe God? If someone asked you, "What is God like?" what would you say? If your picture of God is not biblically accurate, then doubt has fertile soil in which to grow. This second area — an inaccurate view of God — may apply to you.

I have found people who view God as much too small. Their God is so small that the complexities of life baffle their faith.

Other people picture God so narrowly that only

people in their little group have the "corner on truth." Thus, they dare not ask difficult questions.

Still others imagine God as rigid and demanding. This view of a sometimes cruel, even sadistic God kills spontaneity and scares faith into becoming passive.

Yet others take liberties by viewing God as *only* good, loving and compassionate. They fail to incorporate His justice and omnipotence into their picture. Tragically, their God is impotent, and their faith lacks a trustworthy object.

This type of doubt is based on a person's misguided, faulty picture of God. It has nothing to do with what God is *really* like.

Inadequate Theology

Marie, calling long-distance from Wisconsin, desperately relayed her story to me. "I feel so much guilt for doubting. My minister told me doubt is evil and of the devil. I'm so scared. I do real well for a few days, then the doubts come back, stronger than ever. What must God think of me?"

She began to cry and continued, "I try so hard to do everything I'm told in church and to believe everything I'm taught. Do you think God is punishing me because I can't seem to believe? He is probably so disappointed in me."

Marie had been brought up in a rigid, legalistic church. It subtly presented God as demanding, angry and out to get His pound of flesh from sinful, wicked people. Her church's primary means of motivation seemed to be fear and guilt. It was no wonder Marie was confused, frightened and full of doubt. Anyone who came face to face with Marie's God would have doubted.

Faced with erroneous views of God, people have no choice but to doubt. After all, faith is trust. Who can trust a God who is too small, or narrow, or demanding, or impotent? Doubt then becomes protection against such unbiblical notions of God.

Typically, a person trapped in this type of doubt fails to see that his problem lies not in his faith, but in his theology. Thus he turns on his faith and treats it with cruel disdain. "What's wrong with my faith? Why can't I believe?" He tries even harder to force himself to believe these false views. Because his mind cannot embrace this theology, his faith cannot sustain it.

Know Who God Is

The solution to this category of doubt is to develop a biblically accurate view of God. This takes time, due to a number of factors.

First, people commonly reason from themselves to God. For example, "This is what I think love is. Therefore, God's love is just a bigger, more perfect picture of how I love." This can lead to all sorts of unbiblical thinking and acting.

To develop a biblical view of God, you need to reason from God to yourself. Look at how God describes Himself, not at what you think He is like. The two might be radically different. Paul refers to this process of changing our thinking as renewing our minds (Romans 12:2).

Also, it takes time to develop an accurate view of God because a person may not be conscious of his erroneous concepts. He may have inherited his ideas from his parents or culture, or absorbed them as he read philosophy or talked to friends. His faulty views may surface as he is studying the Bible. Or perhaps they will emerge when he is faced with an intolerable emotional response to a life situation. Only after he becomes aware of them can he correct them.

God has revealed Himself specifically through His Son, Jesus Christ, and through His written Word, the Bible. Thus, developing a biblically accurate view of God requires time spent reading the Bible. Begin by slowly reading through the New Testament, recording in a notebook everything that is said about the character of God and of Jesus Christ. Two excellent books, *Knowing God* by J. I. Packer and *Knowledge of the Holy* by A. W. Tozer, also can quickly clear up misconceptions about God.

There may be compounded reasons a person sees God as he does. Some people simply lack correct information, and knowledge usually will solve their problem. Others also have been treated poorly by a respected authority figure, thus causing them to project negative feelings onto God. In those cases, all the reading in the world will not resolve the doubting. They need further assistance, which will be discussed under the category "Damaged Emotions."

Marie, whom I referred to earlier, had tangled

roots to her doubt. She not only lacked correct information about what God was like, but she also had been treated poorly growing up, which fed her incorrect view of God. No wonder she doubted. Marie eventually sought out proper theological and emotional help and began on a road toward knowing God as He really is.

Knowing God is the greatest privilege available to man. Get to know Him as He really is. Let God be God. As you do, freedom will replace bondage, truth will replace error, faith will replace doubt.

Immorality

I had just finished speaking at a conference when a college student asked if she could talk to me. We sat down with coffee and she began pouring out her story. She had myriad problems, including doubt. This disturbed her, as she was helping to provide leadership in a Christian organization on campus. I was amazed at her openness. I also sensed she had a solid foundation to her faith. But something was not right. I continued to listen, puzzled. Then I noticed she had a hard time looking me in the eyes. She would glance at me and then down at the table, as though embarrassed or ashamed.

Finally, I asked a direct question that shocked me as much as it did her. "Are you involved in immorality?"

She began to cry, but I could tell she was relieved. She proceeded to tell me she was involved in an immoral relationship with another woman. The guilt was tearing her apart.

As we talked, she began to see the connection between her doubts and the immorality. We talked at length about God's forgiveness as well as a plan to get her the help she needed. As we parted, I gave her a big hug, and told her how much courage she had to face her problem squarely.

Nothing will deaden the vitality of a person's faith and cause doubts to fester more rapidly than being involved in immorality. The internal conflict of claiming to be a believer, yet directly disobeying God, often surfaces as doubt. It is easier to doubt God than to face the consequences of sin and to stop doing what is causing the conflict. (If you have questions as to what might be considered immoral acts, read 1 Thessalonians 4:3-6; Galatians 5:19-21; and 1 Corinthians 6:9-11).

The guilt feelings that often overwhelm a person engaged in immorality also can translate into doubt. Again, it is less painful to doubt than to admit guilt. Frequently, however, doubt and guilt go hand in hand. Both are experienced simultaneously.

Resolving this type of doubt is relatively easy to explain but not necessarily easy to do: Confess the immorality as sin and stop it!

The apostle John tells us, "If we confess our sins, He is faithful and righteous to forgive us our sins and to cleanse us from all unrighteousness" (1 John 1:9). Confession is more than just saying words; it is agreeing with God that what we are doing is wrong and harmful. The Bible clearly admonishes us to flee or run away from immorality because it is devastating.[7]

There is no question that it is difficult to deal with doubt caused by immorality. Often, the immorality is deeply rooted in emotional issues, making it even more difficult. If this category applies to you, reach out for help. Go to a trusted friend, counselor or pastor for help and guidance.

Immorality and a strong vital faith are in antithesis to each other. To maintain a healthy, growing faith, you need to face and overcome immorality. Doubt can be your comrade in this by forcing you to confront your sin.

It is never too late to start doing what is right. Start now! God's forgiveness and power to restore are available the moment you turn to Him.

Tackling these first three areas of sources of doubt — a faulty foundation, an inaccurate view of God, and immorality — is not easy. The doubter may face a time of studying intensely, changing preconceived notions about God, and making difficult choices. But it is worth it. The apostle Paul implores believers to "fight the good fight of faith" (1 Timothy 6:12). Fighting to develop a faith based on a solid foundation, free from erroneous concepts about God, and rooted in holiness, is what the fight of faith is all about. A person serious about his faith will engage in that fight.

CHAPTER 9

TAKE TWO ASPIRINS AND EAT A BROWNIE!

"I respect faith, but doubt is what gets you an education."
Wilson Mizer[1]

Carolyn Rexius, my mentor and close friend, has one grand solution for anything that ails her family: Take two aspirins and eat a brownie. Now that's my kind of solution!

I vacationed recently with the Rexius family on a houseboat at Lake Shasta. That week every complaint, large or small, prompted that same compassionate response. By the end of the week, no one dared complain about anything . . . unless, of course, they wanted a brownie.

Wouldn't it be wonderful if one solution could

resolve every problem of doubt? Life would be so much easier if we could take two aspirins and eat a brownie, or decide *once and for all* never to doubt again, and *Poof* our doubts would vanish. Of course, it's not that easy.

People caught in the web of doubt are driven to find the answer to: How do I resolve it? How can I make it go away? I'm tired of doubting.

Three sources of doubt were discussed in chapter eight. In this chapter, the remaining four areas will be explained with encouraging, helpful insights for resolving the doubt in each case.

Faith Being Tested

I hate pain. In whatever shape or form pain comes, I could easily do without it. Yet life is full of difficulties, and these difficulties are the very substance used to test our faith, and thus produce endurance. And a faith that endures is what will take us through life triumphantly.

But, here's the rub. When the pressure is the greatest, and the fire the hottest, doubt can invade. It is common, if not normal, for questions and doubts to arise in the darkest times of our lives. How do we handle them?

Perspective.

How we see unpleasant realities makes all the difference in handling this type of doubt. An accurate, biblical perspective is vital.

In the past, I spent hours wishing away difficulties. I wasted an incredible amount of time and energy trying to complain them away. Finally, I accepted that life is difficult, and I began working on my perspective.

A significant change resulted from a speaker's talk on the testing of our faith. I don't remember anything else he said, but I'll never forget his illustration:

"When engineers and contractors have finished a train track over a canyon, do you know what they do?" The speaker smiled and continued. "They take a locomotive weighing tons, drive it out in the middle of the bridge and park it. They leave it there for hours, even days. Do you know why they do that? Not to destroy the bridge they have just painstakingly built, but to test its strength. Their purpose is to find out how strong the bridge is and to locate any weak spots, which could cause a major disaster if not corrected."

I got the point. I actually felt excited as I thought through the implication.

You see, I knew that trials were a part of the Christian life, but my attitude toward them, my perspective, was off just enough to produce problems, particularly doubt. Somewhere I had picked up the notion that God arbitrarily sends trials my way just to see if I will trust Him. The implication is that the troublesome circumstance is all for God's benefit. How wrong I was! God can and does use the trials that are a part of life, but for *our* good. And He uses them not to destroy our faith, but to test the quality of our faith; to test its strength. This is for our benefit. He knows how strong our faith is, but often we don't.

In His mercy, God carefully spotlights weak points in our faith that need attention, so we can avoid a potentially more dangerous consequence later in life.

This perspective freed me to see God as my ally rather than my taskmaster. Slowly, as my outlook began to change, my doubts were replaced by faith.

Spiritual Warfare

Christians are in a battle. The New Testament makes it clear that believers have three battle fronts: the world (1 John 2:15-17), the flesh (Galatians 5:16,17) and Satan (1 Peter 5:8,9; Ephesians 6:10-13). How we fight on each front is crucial. We need to pick our weapons carefully.

In all warfare, different weapons serve different purposes. For example, World War II battleships were equipped with anti-aircraft guns for shooting down enemy planes, torpedoes for sinking enemy ships, and depth charges for dropping on enemy submarines. Now, if an enemy fighter-plane was diving toward the ship, threatening destruction, it would do absolutely no good to drop a depth charge. The right weapon would need to be used on the enemy.

That is exactly how it is in spiritual warfare. We need to use the right biblical weapon as we face each of these three battle fronts.

The weapon God has given us to battle the world's way of thinking and acting is to renew our minds (Romans 12:1,2). This process requires time in God's Word. Renewal involves thinking from God's perspective rather than from man's.

God's sure-fire weapon for dealing with the flesh, particularly immorality, can be summed up in one word: flee! (1 Corinthians 6:18) In the heat of immoral passion, how strategically foolish it would be to pull out the wrong weapon. *Uh oh, I'm in trouble! It's time to renew my mind.* That would be like dropping a depth charge when you need to fire your anti-aircraft gun. Get out of there! Flee! You are not strong enough to resist.

Finally, God's weapon against Satan is to resist him (James 4:7; 1 Peter 5:9). In doing so, we must remember who Satan is: the "father of lies" (John 8:44), the master deceiver. His purpose in the life of the believer is "to steal, and kill, and destroy" (John 10:10). One way he does that is by shooting fiery darts our way (Ephesians 6:16).

Doubt can be one of these darts. If Satan can get us to doubt the character of God or the existence of God, he is well on the way to stealing, killing or destroying our faith.

So how do we resist? Resisting has a passive as well an an active aspect. The passive aspect is to stand firm and to let God do our fighting for us. We are to "be strong in the Lord, and in the strength of His might" (Ephesians 6:10). Although Satan is powerful, there is no question that "greater is He [Jesus Christ] who is in you than he [Satan] who is in the world" (1 John 4:4).

Picture a little boy standing up straight and tall,

his arms folded across his chest, smiling humbly, yet confidently at a big bully. Right behind him is his father, two and a half times his son's size, standing there, powerful, brave and protective. The son is strong in the strength of his father, so he is able to stand firm.

But resisting also has an active aspect. You are to resist by "taking up the shield of faith with which you will be able to extinguish the flaming missiles of the evil one" (Ephesians 6:16).

If faith is taking God at His Word (chapter 2), how do we take up the shield of faith when Satan throws a doubt our way? We deflect it by choosing to believe God's Word over Satan's lie.

Now let's take the analogy of the little boy and his father a step further. Picture the bully taunting the little boy. "Ha, your father doesn't love you!" That's a flaming missile.

Shaken, and with his lower lip beginning to quiver, the little fellow looks up at his father and says, "Dad, I know you've told me before that you love me, but that mean bully scares me. Could I ask again, Dad, do you love me?"

"Yes, son, I love you very much, and it's OK to ask again."

With renewed assurance, the little guy turns back to the bully, crosses his arms, and once again smiles confidently. He has taken his father at his word.

When Satan throws a fiery missile our way that mockingly says "God doesn't love you!" we can put up our shield of faith by taking our Father at His

Word. We can say, "Father, I'm beginning to doubt Your love and I need reassurance. Thank You that Jeremiah 31:3 says You have loved me with an everlasting love."

Very simply, this is what it means to resist Satan. And God promises that if we resist Satan, he will flee from us.[2] Learning to resist requires patience and time. And like the little boy, we need constant reassurance of the truth of God's Word.

It is easy to attribute a problem such as doubt *all* to Satan. And nothing terrifies a struggling doubter more than to be told he is either oppressed or possessed by demons. Yet that is exactly what well-meaning advisors frequently say. This only increases the doubter's sense of fear and helplessness, since he already secretly fears it is true. He begins to think, *If only I could get these demons cast out, then my doubts would be gone.* Unconsciously he looks for a quick fix, which only perpetuates his spiritual, intellectual and emotional immaturity.

How do I know? Did I ever wonder if I was demon-possessed? You bet! When emotional turmoil becomes intolerable, you wonder anything. And this is a common fear for people trapped in doubt. Yet, to my knowledge, I have never met or talked to anyone struggling with doubt who was genuinely demon-possessed.

So be careful when assessing the source of doubt. Satan is a powerful foe, and he can and does use doubt as a weapon, but to give him too much credit is foolish.

Damaged Emotions

Os Guinness states that "battered emotions can produce a crop of doubts just as devastating as the militant athiests' toughest questions."[3]

Doubts that arise out of damaged emotions can be among the most difficult to resolve. They are incredibly painful, needing tender, compassionate attention.

As stated earlier, faith is trust. The faith needed for salvation is a gift from God. He delights to give this saving faith to anyone who wants to know Him.

The ability to trust another person emotionally, however, is a gift parents give to their children. Emotional trust is learned early in life through the parent-child relationship. As a child relates to his parents, he learns that it is safe to trust. He discovers that the object of his dependence is trustworthy. He experiences what it's like to rest emotionally in the arms of a good, loving parent, and he begins to internalize that emotion.

As he grows, a child continually tests and reinforces his early experience. This, then, becomes the basis for the child's ability to emotionally trust other people, the world around him, and eventually God. This is why God puts such a high premium on the family. A person's experience in his first and primary trust relationship either enhances or hinders his ability to trust God on an emotional level.

With this type of doubt, the issue is not whether God has or hasn't given a person saving faith. That became his the moment he asked Christ into his life.

The issue is the believer's ability to lean or depend upon God on a feeling level. What is at stake is not salvation but the believer's emotional sense of safety and security.

If the parents, the child's first trust objects, were aloof, indifferent, emotionally cold, abusive, cruel, hostile, untrustworthy, etc., the child will have difficulty emotionally trusting others, including God. His subconscious mind will be filled with the hurt from damaged emotions and the inability to trust. This unexpressed hurt can slowly begin to make itself heard in the form of doubt. Or when a crisis hits or something taps into these buried emotions, the lid blows off. Savagely, the emotions rise up to conquer faith and reason, and doubt reigns supreme.

It is difficult to describe the emotional agony of this experience. My heart goes out to anyone in the midst of this kind of turmoil. And I know only too well that "thinking right" won't stop it. Legalistic Bible reading or praying doesn't work either. Trying to get the lid back on your feelings is futile. Deciding never to doubt again is as ludicrous as it is impossible.

How does a person know if his doubts are emotionally based? The following questions may help you determine if this is your problem.

1. Are your doubts obsessive? In other words, are they difficult to stop even when you have reasonable answers to your questions?
2. Do you doubt your salvation?
3. Are you overly concerned as to whether you committed the "unpardonable sin"?
4. Are you wanting to believe with all your heart,

yet unable to stop the doubts?

5. Are you afraid you might be demon-possessed?
6. Do your doubts center on unanswerable questions? (I.e., Who is the author of evil? Why did God create man if He knew he would sin? How can God allow suffering?)
7. Are you experiencing anxiety, guilt and fear?
8. When you read the Bible, do you feel condemned?
9. Do you have a hard time sleeping?
10. Are you too hard on yourself?
11. Do you set high standards for yourself, bordering on perfectionism?
12. Do you feel helpless? Have you tried everything to stop your doubts and found that nothing has worked?

If you answered "yes" to some or all of these questions, then your doubt may be emotionally based. This does not mean no other issues are involved, but the root of your doubt probably is emotional.

So what should you do? You need to find healing, but where do you begin?

First, take the pressure off yourself by recognizing that your problem is not with God or with your faith; rather, it is with your damaged emotions.

Second, focus on finding healing for those deep emotional wounds, not on answering all the questions screaming at you from your doubts. Focusing on the doubts only takes energy away from dealing with the real emotional issue.

Third, be good to yourself. Likely, you are your

own worst enemy. Instead of being hard on yourself, cultivate a pattern of treating your feelings with care and respect. Your feelings are you.

Fourth, read books that address this tender and sensitive issue (see the suggested reading list).

Fifth, seek help from a respected Christian counselor or psychologist. The hurt you've experienced may be too deep to be handled adequately by a lay person.

Finally, continue to cultivate a correct view of God.

Emotionally based doubts are the most painful. They are torture! You may be tempted to throw in the towel. Progress may seem too slow — you want to stop the doubts *now!*

Yet, you cannot take a short cut to emotional healing, because there are none. It took time to get where you are and it will take time to undo the damage.

"But can't God heal instantly?" you may ask. I believe He can and does heal immediately on occasion, but He usually allows us to go through the normal healing process of life.

For instance, let's say I broke my leg. God could instantly heal it, but more than likely I would need to have it set and casted. My leg would then mend through the magnificent healing process God placed within my body. I believe it's the same with emotional healing. God could have healed me instantly, but He didn't. He allowed me to go through a healing process, resulting in growth toward wholeness and health.

So don't give up! Multitudes of believers from throughout the ages are cheering you on. Most important, God is on your side. He is committed to your wholeness. He is the author and sustainer of your faith. Your faith will not fail.

The Normal Growth Process

Life is growth. To possess life is to possess an inner urge to stretch, learn, change, feel, move ahead, love, create — to grow. Growth implies process. This process involves successes, which exhilarate the soul, and failures, which shatter our dreams. Both experiences are involved in our constant growth.

The Christian life is no exception, although for a time I thought I could be the first exception. Like a child who can barely wait to grow up, I wanted to be instantly mature, knowing everything older Christians knew. I found myself frustrated at what I didn't know and pushing myself to learn faster. Then the question hit me: Would you rather be a squash or an oak tree?

I had read that it takes six weeks to produce a squash, but it takes a hundred years to produce an oak tree. I got the picture. Growing into maturity takes a lifetime. So I began to settle into the growth process. However, I subconsciously exempted from this growth process one dimension of my life: my faith. Subtly I put it into a category all its own. Of course, I knew faith grew the more you used it. But to me that meant I went from believing God for smaller matters to believing Him for bigger ones. It left no room for doubts or questions. Failure was not even entertained.

My fantasy was short-lived . . . and I'm glad. Embracing reality, though difficult, always leads to maturity. The reality is that our faith is subject to the growth process, just like every other area of our lives. Doubt is a normal part of this growth. At times we doubt ourselves, our decisions, God's leading, perhaps even His intentions. But when we wrestle with these doubts and come out the victor, we find our faith has grown. Even more astounding, we are more sure of God.

This last area of doubt sources can actually encompass the other six. They *all* are a part of the growth process. Thus, there is no specific solution for this type of doubt; the issue is too broad. All of the earlier solutions can be applied, however, according to your particular need.

Most important, embrace growth. When you do, you embrace life.

So, how do you solve the problem of doubt? Come to my house — I'll make the brownies and get the aspirins! No, it is not that simple. Resolving doubt takes time, but it is possible. Doubt need not master you. It can, in fact, serve you as you build a vital faith.

CHAPTER 10

THE MAKING OF
A BELIEVER

"I spent a long time trying to come to grips
with my doubts and suddenly I realized that
I had better come to grips with what I believe.
I have since moved from the agony of questions
that I cannot answer to the reality of answers
that I cannot escape . . . and it's a great relief."
Tom Skinner[1]

Labeling people is as unfair as it is cruel.
That's why I vote we change the name of Doubting
Thomas to Honest Thomas. Through the centuries,
this poor man has been unjustly tagged as the stubborn, doubting disciple. But on the contrary, Thomas
did what most intelligent people would have done
in this situation: He asked for justifiable evidence.

In John 20:19-29, we read that Jesus appeared
to the disciples after His resurrection and showed
them the nail prints in His hands and His pierced
side. The disciples were overjoyed that this was
indeed their risen Lord! But Thomas was not there

to see the proof. (I can't help but wonder if he felt a little hurt and left out.)

When Thomas arrived, the others reported the unbelievable news — Jesus was alive! They already had seen and examined Him. They *knew* He was alive. But until that very moment, Thomas had believed Jesus was dead. Suddenly he was confronted with excited men announcing this incredulous news. I imagine Thomas was on overload with too many new thoughts and feelings all at once.

I am not surprised Thomas wanted the same proof his friends had received. He, too, wanted to see Jesus. I believe the disciple was demonstrating intellectual integrity at this point.

The following eight days must have seemed an eternity to Thomas. Finally Jesus appeared, and Thomas actually saw the Lord with his own eyes. Jesus freely gave His questioning follower the evidence he so desperately needed. I can almost sense Thomas's humility, awe and immediate belief as he cried out, "My Lord and my God!" (verse 28)

Why did the Lord have John record this account of Thomas? Was it to show us the failure of a doubter? I don't believe so. I have a hunch He wanted us to observe the making of a believer.

God is in the business of making believers. This process is etched on every page of the Bible. Making believers is also the ultimate focus of this book. A book on doubt must, by necessity, come full circle back to faith — that indispensible quality necessary for successful Christian living. For what is doubt resolved if it is not faith increased? And a maturing believer is one who keeps faith in proper focus.

Faith in Focus

The young man surprised me when he interrupted my reading and said, "I noticed you reading the Bible. Do you mind if I sit down and talk a minute?"

Not wanting to be rude, I motioned for him to join me.

His minute stretched into the remaining hour of my flight. A missionary with his particular religion, he was intent on persuading me to his point of view. I felt sad as I observed his dedication to a system of belief based on works: man's efforts to find acceptance with God.

Finally he asked for my response to his ideas. I answered, "Thank you for sharing your experience. I can tell it means a lot to you and you are deeply sincere. However, I am unable to agree. You see, I believe all of the Scriptures assert that my acceptance with God comes through faith in the finished work of Christ on the cross for me. My faith rests in Jesus Christ alone and nothing else."

As we cordially parted ways, I sensed this young man's frustration with his failure to persuade me to his beliefs. Once again, the eternal distinction between Christianity and every other religion was clear to me: Salvation is through faith alone, not works. What freedom!

Evangelicals today are united and strong on this one issue. We cringe whenever anyone asserts that we have to "do something" to obtain salvation. That suggestion throws up an immediate red flag. We pull out Bible verses, argue adamantly for, and protect vehemently the doctrine of salvation through faith alone, and rightly so.

Yet over the years I've observed a subtle phenomenon that concerns me. Faith seems to have become the evangelicals' "work." When that happens, faith is out of focus.

It goes like this: We know the only thing that qualifies us for salvation is trust in what Jesus Christ accomplished for us on Calvary. What He accomplished becomes ours by faith: "By grace you have been saved through faith" (Ephesians 2:8).

But here is the subtle danger. We focus on possessing faith rather than on what Christ has done. Faith, we reason, is a tangible "thing" we need to secure, offer to God and, as a result, receive what He has for us. We begin to look internally for something that can come only from God. At times we frantically cry out, "I need to have more faith." Unconsciously, we are asking, "What internal thing can I do to activate God?" This is another way of asking, "How can I be in control?"

Faith is not a ticket we possess to get us into God's favor. It is simply a response to what God has offered. Faith is receiving. It is humility, for we offer nothing to God, yet we receive all He has for us. Faith has nothing to do with a quality possessed, but rather it is a choice to receive and respond to all that God already has accomplished.

Hudson Taylor captured this concept when he

questioned, "How then to have our faith increased? Only by thinking of all that Jesus is and all He is for us: His life, His death, His work, He Himself as revealed to us in the Word, to be the subject of our constant thoughts. Not striving to have faith . . . but a looking off to the faithful one seems all we need; a resting in the Loved One entirely, for time and for eternity,"[2]

This is faith in focus.

Will the Real God Please Stand Up?

J. I. Packer writes, "What makes life worthwhile is having a big enough objective, something which catches our imagination and lays hold of our allegiance; and this the Christian has, in a way that no other man has. For what higher, more exalted, and more compelling goal can there be than to know God?"[3]

Knowing God — knowing Him as He really is — is the key ingredient in the making of a believer. But that ingredient is lacking in the lives of many Christians in our country. These individuals may be seeking such knowledge, but for the most part they are not finding it in the churches they attend. Many leave their services more confused than when they entered because of the profusion of ideas and concepts proposed about God. They wonder, "Who do I believe? Everyone seems to say something different about God. Will the real God please stand up?"

The confusion and misperceptions seem to result from our propensity to project onto God what we think He should be, or what we wish He would be, or what our particular society proclaims Him to be, rather than seeing God as He has revealed Himself in His Word.

This tendency begins early in life. If you ask a child what God is like, his answer probably will reflect how he views his parents, and what particular stage of growth he is in. Thus, his perspective will change with each developmental stage. God becomes an extension of his internal world.

For instance, a young child might view God as an extension of himself; He is there to meet his needs as the child wills. As he grows older, he could potentially view god as the Mighty Warrior, stamping out all bad. When evil remains, he feels disappointed in his conqueror. If a child has been hurt and treated without respect, he probably will experience God as cruel and inconsiderate of his feelings or needs; someone ready to use him but not to love him.

After I became a Christian, I unconsciously projected onto God an image of someone who would fulfill all my hopes, dreams, unmet needs and longings repressed from a painful childhood. I failed to see God as He really is; a Being separate from me with a will that is higher than and different from mine yet who is committed to my good.

I wanted God to rescue me out of my pain and "make everything all right." Instead, He walked with me in and through my hurt, allowing me to feel my anger and to grieve, eventually opening the door for forgiveness and the ability to receive all that was available to me from Him and from others. In the process, my faith matured.

Growing up is a painful process. Just as a child eventually separates from his parents and begins to see them as they really are, so too a maturing Christian will come to the point of separating from his projected image of God. That will open the door to knowing God as He really is.

It is important to understand that we can never know God through our senses or imaginings. He has revealed what He is like through His Son and through His written Word, the Bible. If we want to know God as He really is, we will find Him in the face of Jesus Christ and across the pages of Scripture.

As this process of maturity begins, we may feel a tremendous sense of loss. It is always difficult to give up projected hopes and wishes. But the result will be well worth the price paid. We now can build a relationship based on truth and reality. Instead of trying to control God, we can begin to experience Him in all of His magnificence, beauty, grace and power. The longed-for intimacy of Creator to creation, Father to child, and Friend to friend begins to grow and develop. As J. I. Packer says, "Knowing God is a relationship calculated to thrill a man's heart."[4] When the real God stands up, it is certain that "every knee will bow . . . and every tongue confess that Jesus Christ is Lord" (Philippians 2:10,11).

A Time To Believe

In every doubter's life there comes a point when it is time to believe. This is another dimension of the making of a believer. He chooses to move from living in the state of double-mindedness to living in the state of faith. This choice is not made prematurely, but only when the doubter has adequately resolved the root of his particular type of doubt. And making such a decision does not mean he will never doubt again; it just means he is changing from a state of doubt to one of faith.

The circumstances surrounding the choice to believe will look different in each individual life. Thomas's time to believe came when he examined the evidence. For Moses it came after his faulty view of how God works was corrected. Job made his choice after his faith was tested and he learned to suspend judgment and live with mystery. Billy Graham's time to believe came one evening while walking alone at a retreat site before his 1949 Crusade. After struggling with the question of the inerrancy of Scripture, he knelt down and made a choice to believe based on evidence that the Bible is, indeed, the inerrant Word of God.

I admire few people as I do Joni Eareckson Tada. Her courage and faith will forever be a model to me of God's grace. Her time to believe is wrapped up in her personal heart-rending story.

A vibrant, active, athletic teenager, Joni's life was dramatically and instantly changed in 1967 with one dive into the Chesapeake Bay. "I felt the pull of the water . . . and then a stunning jolt . . . My head crashed into a rock on the bottom. My limbs splayed out. I felt a loud buzzing, like an electric shock accompanied by intense vibration. Yet there was no pain.

"I couldn't move! My face was pressing against

the grinding sand on the bottom but I couldn't get up. My mind was directing my muscles to swim but nothing responded. I held my breath, prayed, and waited, suspended face-down in the water."[5]

At that moment, Joni became a quadraplegic. During the following three years, she experienced a depth of agony few people ever face. "At first, Joni found her condition impossible to reconcile with her faith in a loving God. It seemed all God's gifts, the good things she had enjoyed as an active teenager, had been stolen from her. What did she have left?

"The turning to God was slow. Change from bitterness to trust in Him dragged out over three years of tears and violent questionings."[6]

Joni's time to believe began when a friend, desperately trying to be a comfort, hesitatingly pointed out that Jesus, too, had been paralyzed on the cross. He understood her pain. Slowly, Joni began pondering that thought. It became a great comfort to her. *He knows; He cares.* This was the beginning of Joni's choice to believe.

"Few of us have the luxury — it took me forever to think of it as that — to come to ground zero with God. Before the accident, my questions had always been 'How will God fit into this situation? How will He affect my dating life? My career plans? The things I enjoy?' All those options were gone. It was me, just a helpless body, and God.

"I had no other identity but God, and gradually He became enough.

"My focus changed from demanding an explanation from God to humbly depending on Him."[7]

I remember sitting in a packed auditorium listening to Joni speak. In my own pain, I felt comfort as I clung to every word she said. *If God can do for me internally what I see He's done for her, then there's hope.*

Thousands of people have come from far and wide to hear Joni speak and sing. Her art work, done with a brush held in her teeth, is found in stores across the country. Joni went from being an active teenager, through the stage of being a helpless, suicidal quadraplegic, on to becoming a vibrant woman with a ministry that reaches worldwide — all from the confines of a wheelchair. I am confident the impact of this one young woman, who while lying helpless in a hospital bed decided it was time to believe, will be felt throughout eternity.

The Crossroad

I will never forget my time to believe. After struggling with my doubts for a number of years, I came to the crossroad. My greatest fear was that someday I would lose my faith. But I didn't care anymore. Lying on my couch crying bitterly, I yelled out, "OK, God, I'm tired of trying to believe. I'm tired of the pain and confusion and doubt. If You're not going to help me out of this, then I'm through believing."

In anger and hurt, I continued, "From now on, I don't believe there is a God. You do not exist. There is *no* God."

(Looking back, I smile when I think of this

conversation I had with the person I didn't believe existed anymore.)

For three days, I angrily walked around trying to convince myself I didn't believe. Without knowing it, I was experiencing God's grace, for one aspect of His grace is the guarantee that He will preserve me; that my future as His child is assured.[8] I discovered that the Christian, as Packer writes, "need not torment himself with the fear that his faith may fail; as grace led him to faith in the first place, so grace will keep him believing to the end."[9]

At the end of those three days, I was still angry — but also relieved. As hard as I tried *not* to believe, I discovered I could not stop believing. I believed! I had faced my greatest fear squarely, and the relief was overwhelming. Once again, I talked to God. "OK, Lord, I do believe. Forgive me for my attitude. I guess the question is not, Is there a God? but it is, How in the world do I relate to You? Would You show me?"

My choice to believe put me on the road to knowing God as He really is. Do I ever doubt anymore? Yes. But the doubts no longer have the same emotional power in my life. The freedom and growth that followed my choice to believe have been well worth the years of struggle.

Dealing with your doubts may be the most difficult but important step you will ever take in your Christian life. Embrace the process. And, after you apply all the reasoning, analyzing and suggestions, the ultimate answer to your doubts will lie in your personal, inner knowledge of Jesus Christ. You will discover that doubt *is* a road to growth.

THE "UNPARDONABLE SIN"

Henry Cloud, Ph.D.

Many times people who are struggling with doubt question their salvation and the security of their relationship with the Lord. They feel that they have "lost their salvation," either by some act or thought, or by God's rejection of them from His family. Although the sources of these fears are many, often they relate to the passages in the Gospels where Jesus talks of an "eternal sin," which He calls the blasphemy of the Holy Spirit. It is important to understand what that exactly means.

The incident surrounding this saying is reported in Matthew, Mark and Luke. As we see in Matthew, it involved Jesus' display of His deity by casting out demons. The Pharisees, in typical fashion, rejected the truth of what He had done, and tried to come up with some alternative explanation for how He did it. They could not deny that power had been present, for the man was cured. So, instead of acknowledging that it was the power of God, they said that it was the power of Satan.

To understand what this particular sin is and why it was unforgivable, we must understand the role of the Holy Spirit in the ministry of Jesus, then and now. It is the job of the Spirit to reveal to man who Jesus really is, i.e., that He is God and the way of salvation. John 16:8-11 tells us that He "convicts the world concerning sin, and righteousness, and judgment; *concerning sin because they do not believe in [Him];* and concerning righteousness, because [He goes] to the Father, and you no longer behold [Him]; and concerning judgment, because the ruler of this world has been judged." It is very easy to see this function of the Spirit in this example. He was showing the Pharisees that Jesus was who He said He was by this obvious display of power. The only reason it was unforgivable, or as Jesus says in Mark 3:29, that one who does not recognize the Spirit's teaching "never has forgiveness," is that to recognize who Jesus is is the only way to be forgiven. That is why it was unforgivable; it is the sin of unbelief. To refuse to see who Jesus is places one outside the only possible arena of forgiveness, which is belief in Him. Thus, "He who believes in Him is not judged; he who does not believe has been judged already, because he has not believed in the name of the only begotten Son of God" (John 3:18). That is why in the Matthew account Jesus makes the statement, "He who is not with Me is against Me; and he who does not gather with Me scatters" (Matthew 12:30).

It is Satan's best trick to try to confuse a believer about his or her salvation, because it undermines the security that one has in the Lord. Revelation calls Satan the "accuser of the brethren . . . who accuses them before our God day and night" (Revelation 12:10). If he tries to make you doubt your salvation, do what Jesus did and quote the Word of God. "Truly, truly I say to you, he who believes has eternal life" (John 6:47).

If one fears that he has committed this unpardonable sin, the best proof that he has not is that fear itself, for it shows a heart that knows who Jesus is and one that wants to belong to Him. If one wants forgiveness for anything, that shows that God is drawing that person to Himself and that He will not reject him. "No one can come to Me, unless the Father who sent Me draws him; and I will raise him up on the last day. All that the Father gives Me shall come to Me, and the one who comes to Me I will certainly not cast out. And this is the will of Him who sent Me, that of all He has given Me I lose nothing, but raise it up on the last day" (John 6:44,37,39). Rest assured, "God is not a man, that He should lie, nor a son of man that He should repent; has He said, and will He not do it? Or has He spoken, and will He not make it good?" (Numbers 23:19)

SUGGESTED READING LIST

I. The Attributes of God:

The God of All Comfort, Hannah Whitall Smith, Moody Press

The Knowledge of the Holy, A. W. Tozer, Harper and Row

Knowing God, J. I. Packer, InterVarsity Press

Majesty! The God You Should Know, J. Sidlow Baxter, Here's Life Publishers

II. Biographies:

Charles H. Spurgeon, W. Y. Fullerton, Moody Press

Created for Commitment, A. Wetherall Johnson, Tyndale House

Fanny Crosby, Sandy Deugler, Moody Press

Francis Schaeffer, Louis G. Parkhurst, Jr., Tyndale House

George Mueller, Basil Miller, Bethany House

The Hiding Place, Corrie Ten Boom, Chosen Books

Hudson Taylor's Spiritual Secret, Dr. and Mrs. Howard Taylor, Moody Press

Joni, Joni Eareckson, Zondervan

The Life of D. L. Moody, A. P. Fitt, Moody Press

Shadow of the Almighty, Elisabeth Elliot,
  Zondervan
Surprised by Joy, C. S. Lewis, Harcourt,
  Brace and Jovanovich

III.   Christian Apologetics:

An Introduction to Christian Apologetics,
  Edward Campbell, Eerdmans
Answers to Tough Questions, Josh
  McDowell and Don Stewart, Here's
  Life Publishers
The Basis of Christian Faith, Floyd Hamil-
  ton, Harper and Row
Christian Apologetics, Norman Geisler,
  Baker
Escape From Reason, Francis Schaeffer,
  InterVarsity Press
Evangelism and the Sovereignty of God,
  J. I. Packer, InterVarsity Press
*Evidence That Demands A Verdict, Vols.
  I & II,* Josh McDowell, Here's Life
  Publishers
God's Foreknowledge and Man's Free Will,
  Richard Rice, Bethany House
God Who Is There, Francis Schaeffer, Inter-
  Varsity Press
History and Christianity, John W. Montgom-
  ery, InterVarsity Press
Inerrancy, Norman Geisler, Zondervan
Know Why You Believe, Paul Little, Scrip-
  ture Press
*Reasons Skeptics Should Consider Christ-
  ianity,* Josh McDowell and Don

Stewart, Here's Life Publishers

The Resurrection Factor, Josh McDowell, Here's Life Publishers

Who Moved the Stone? Frank Morison, Zondervan

IV. Christian Growth

Authentic Christianity, Ray Stedman, Word Books

The Christian's Secret of a Happy Life, Hannah Whitall Smith, Fleming H. Revell Company

Faith Is Not A Feeling, Ney Bailey, Here's Life Publishers

The Holy Spirit, Bill Bright, Here's Life Publishers

Principles of Spiritual Growth, Miles Stanford, Zondervan

The Pursuit of God, A. W. Tozer, Christian Publications, Inc.

Three Steps Forward, Two Steps Back, Chuck Swindoll, Bantam

The Transferable Concepts, Bill Bright, Here's Life Publishers

V. Doubt:

In Two Minds, Os Guinness, InterVarsity Press

VI. Emotional Healing and Growth:

The Art of Understanding Yourself, Cecil Osborne, Zondervan

Cutting Loose, Howard M. Halpern, Ph.D., Bantam

The Drama of the Gifted Child, Alice Miller, Basic Books Inc.

Effective Biblical Counseling, Lawrence Crabb, Zondervan

Facing Anger, Rohrer and Sutherland, Augsburg Publishing House

Freedom From Guilt, Narramore and Counts, Vision House Publishers

Healing for Damaged Emotions, David Seamonds, Victor Books

No Condemnation, Bruce Narramore, Academic Books

Put It All Together, Maurice Wagner, Zondervan

The Road Less Traveled, M. Scott Peck, A Touchstone Book

The Sensation of Being Somebody, Maurice Wagner, Zondervan

VII.   Foundational Christian Truth:

Basic Christianity, John Stott, InterVarsity Press

Know What You Believe, Paul Little, Scripture Press

Mere Christianity, C. S. Lewis, Macmillan Publishing Co.

The Normal Christian Life, Watchman Nee, Tyndale House

The Ten Basic Steps Toward Christian Maturity, Bill Bright, Here's Life Publishers

VIII.   Spiritual Warfare

The Adversary, Mark Bubeck, Moody Press
Are Demons Real? Robert Peterson, Moody Press
Demonology, Past and Present, Kurt Koch, Kregel Press
Overcoming the Adversary, Mark Bubeck, Moody Press
The Screwtape Letters, C. S. Lewis, Macmillan Publishing Company

IX.   Suffering and Evil:

Affliction, Edith Schaeffer, Fleming H. Revell
Arguing With God: A Christian Examination of the Problem of Evil, Hugh Silvester, InterVarsity Press
Evil and the Love of God, John Hick, Harper and Row
God and Evil, Williams Fitch, Eerdmans
God, Freedom, and Evil, Alvin Platinga, Harper and Row
The Goodness of God, John Wenham, InterVarsity Press
A Grief Observed, C. S. Lewis, Seabury
Mourning Song, Joyce Landorf, Fleming H. Revell
The Problem of Pain, C. S. Lewis, Macmillan Publishing Company
The Roots of Evil, Norman Geisler, Zondervan

Where Is God When It Hurts? Philip Yancey, Zondervan

X.   Miscellaneous:

Christianity and Comparative Religion, J. N. D. Anderson, InterVarsity Press

Christianity and the Problem of Origins, Philip E. Hughes, Baker

Evolution or Creation, Bolton Davidheiser, Baker

God and Philosophy, Anthony Flew, Dell Publishing Company

Introduction to Philosophy: A Christian Perspective, Norman Geisler and Paul Feinberg, Baker

The Christian View of Science and Scripture, Bernard Ramm, Eerdmans

NOTES

Chapter One
1. Wanda Malette and Patti Ryan, "Just Another Woman in Love," Combine Music Corporation, Nashville. Used by permission.
2. E. Stanley Jones, *The Unshakable Kingdom and the Unchanging Person* (Nashville, TN: Abingdon Press, 1972), p. 141.
3. Martin Luther, *What Luther Says: An Anthology,* ed., Ewald M. Plass (St. Louis: Concordia, 1959), p. 426.
4. Os Guinness, *In Two Minds,* (Downers Grove, IL: InterVarsity Press, 1976), p. 43.
5. Ibid., p. 34.
6. Ibid., p. 17.
7. Ibid., p. 63.
8. Larry A. Hjelle and Daniel J. Ziegler, *Personality Theories* (New York: McGraw-Hill Book Company, 1981), p. 400.
9. Elisabeth Elliot, *The Liberty of Obedience* (Waco, TX: Word Books, 1968), p. 16.
10. Ibid., back cover.

Chapter Two
1. B. Bartner, "Distinguish Doubt," in *The New International Dictionary of New Testament Theology,* ed. Colin Brown, 3 vols. (Grand Rapids, MI: Zondervan, 1975), 1:505.
2. Os Guinness, *In Two Minds* (Downers Grove, IL: InterVarsity Press, 1976), p. 25.
3. Ibid., p. 24.

4. Ibid., p. 25.
5. Ibid.
6. Ibid., p. 27.
7. Ibid., p. 28.
8. Peter H. Davids, *The Epistle of James, The New International Greek Testament Commentary* (Grand Rapids, MI: William B. Eerdmans, 1982), p. 74.
9. James Hardy Ropes, *A Critical and Exegetical Commentary on the Epistle of St. James, The International Critical Commentary* (Edinburgh: T. and T. Clark, 1916), p. 143.
10. James B. Adamson, *The Epistle of James, The New International Commentary on the New Testament* (Grand Rapids, MI: William B. Eerdmans, 1976), p. 60.
11. Ibid.
12. Guinness, *Minds,* p. 28.
13. Matthew 13:58.
14. See Mark 9:17-27.
15. Mark 9:24
16. Ropes, *Epistle of St. James,* p. 140.

Chapter Three
1. Os Guinness, *In Two Minds* (Downers Grove, IL: InterVarsity Press, 1976), p. 39.
2. Ibid., p. 35.
3. Cyril J. Barber and Gary Strauss, *Leadership: The Dynamics of Success* (Greenwood, SC: Attic Press, 1982), pp. 25-59. (The section entitled "And Great Was Their Fall" is primarily summary of pp. 25-59. No other footnote will be added except for direct quotes.)

4. See James 1:4.
5. Barber and Strauss, *Leadership,* p. 29.
6. Guinness, *Minds,* p. 44.
7. Lawrence J. Crabb, *Effective Biblical Counseling* (Grand Rapids, MI: Zondervan, 1977), p. 108.
8. Barber and Strauss, *Leadership,* p. 58.
9. Ibid., p. 44.
10. Ibid., p. 59.

Chapter Four
1. Os Guinness, *In Two Minds* (Downers Grove, IL: InterVarsity Press, 1976), p. 16.
2. There are absolutes in life, but not as many as I thought. For me, knowing that Jesus Christ is God, that the Bible is His Word, and that I have forgiveness of sins and eternal life because of my acceptance of Christ's substitutionary death for me, are absolutes on which I base my life. These absolutes are crucial, for they give me the security to face life as it really is. However, apart from these foundational truths, I have learned I cannot afford to be dogmatic.
3. Guinness, *Minds,* p. 254.
4. Ibid., p. 255.
5. See Matthew 11:10.
6. Matthew 14:3.
7. Guinness, *Minds,* p. 259.
8. Ibid., p. 261.
9. Augustine, *Confessions* (Harmondsworth, England: Penguin, 1961), p. 84.
10. Exodus 2:11-15.
11. Genesis 16.
12. Guinness, *Minds,* p. 284.

13. Ibid., p. 285.
14. Ibid., p. 286.
15. Ibid.
16. Genesis 6.
17. Guinness, *Minds,* p. 254.

Chapter Five
 1. C. S. Lewis, *The Problem of Pain* (New York: Macmillan Publishing Co., Inc., 1978), p. 93.
 2. Lewis, *Problem of Pain,* p. 26.
 3. John Gage Allee, Ph.D., ed., *Webster's Dictionary* (Farmingham, MA: Dennison Manufacturing Co., 1977), p. 248.
 4. See Colossians 1:27.
 5. See Ephesians 1:9.
 6. Ray Stedman, *Authentic Christianity* (Waco, TX: Word Books, 1977), p. 47.
 7. Os Guinness, *In Two Minds* (Downers Grove, IL: InterVarsity Press, 1976), p. 257.
 8. See Romans 8:28.
 9. Lewis, *Problem of Pain,* p. 75.
10. A. W. Tozer, *The Knowledge of the Holy* (New York: Harper and Row Publishers, 1961), p. 110.
11. Philip Yancey, *Where Is God When It Hurts?* (Grand Rapids, MI: Zondervan, 1977), p. 54.
12. Lewis, *Problem of Pain,* p. 69.
13. See Job 40:8.
14. Tozer, *Knowledge of the Holy,* p. 113.
15. Lewis, *Problem of Pain,* p. 95.
16. Rev. Marie M. Fortune, "Suffering: To Endure or To Transform?" *Working Together* 4, No. 2 (November/December 1983), n.p.

Chapter Six
1. John 16:33.
2. See Luke 22:31-34.
3. Erwin Lutzer, *Failure: The Back Door to Success* (Chicago: Moody Press, 1975), p. 19.
4. J. I. Packer, *Knowing God* (Downers Grove, IL: InterVarsity Press, 1973), pp. 222-23.
5. See Job 1:12.
6. See Luke 22:31,32.
7. Hannah Whitall Smith, *The Christian's Secret of a Happy Life* (Old Tappan, NJ: Fleming H. Revell Company, 1972), pp. 102-03.
8. See Luke 22:32.
9. See Psalm 144:2.
10. See Hebrews 13:5.
11. See John 17:20.

Chapter Seven
1. Hannah Whitall Smith, *The Christian's Secret of a Happy Life* (Old Tappan, NJ: Fleming H. Revell Company, 1972), p. 123.
2. Ibid.
3. Galatians 5:2-4.
4. Galatians 5:5.
5. Smith, *Christian's Secret,* pp. 113, 116.
6. Ray C. Stedman, *Authentic Christianity* (Waco, TX: Word Books, 1977), p. 88.
7. Smith, *Christian's Secret,* pp. 113-14.
8. Elisabeth Elliot, *The Liberty of Obedience* (Waco, TX: Word Books, 1968), pp. 45-46.
9. See Galatians 5:16,18.
10. Miles J. Stanford, *The Green Letters* (Hong Kong: Living Spring Press, n.d.), p. 5.

11. See Philippians 4:19.

Chapter Eight
 1. Blaise Pascal, *The Pensées,* trans. with introduction by J. M. Cohen (Harmondsworth, England: Penguin, 1961), p. 274.
 2. Cyril Barber, Library Consultant, Campus Crusade for Christ, San Bernardino, CA. Interview, 31 January 1984. (Dr. Barber received his doctorate in marriage and family ministry from Talbot Theological Seminary. He has authored fifteen books.)
 3. See Matthew 7:26,27.
 4. Guinness, *Minds,* p. 103.
 5. Ibid., p. 115.
 6. Fenelon as quoted in *The Christian's Secret of a Happy Life,* Hannah Whitall Smith (Old Tappan, NJ: Fleming H. Revell Company, 1972), p. 57.
 7. See 1 Corinthians 6:18.

Chapter Nine
 1. Lawrence J. Peter, *Peter's Quotations, Ideas for Our Time* (New York: William Morrow & Co., Inc., 1977), p. 167.
 2. See James 4:7.
 3. Os Guinness, *In Two Minds,* (Downers Grove, IL: InterVarsity Press, 1976), p. 158.

Chapter Ten
 1. Tom Skinner, Tom Skinner Associates, New York. Used by permission.
 2. Dr. and Mrs. Howard Taylor, *Hudson Taylor's*

Spiritual Secret (Chicago: Moody Press, 1982), p. 156.

3. J. I. Packer, *Knowing God* (Downers Grove, IL: InterVarsity Press, 1973), p. 30.
4. Ibid., p. 32.
5. Joni Eareckson Tada as quoted in *Where Is God When It Hurts?* Philip Yancey (Grand Rapids, MI: Zondervan, 1977), p. 113.
6. Ibid., p. 118.
7. Ibid., p. 119.
8. Packer, *Knowing God,* p. 123.
9. Ibid.